LEADING TO
DISASTER

LEADING TO DISASTER

SCOTT MACAULAY

ISBN, paperback: 978-1-80227-206-2
ISBN, ebook: 978-1-80227-207-9
ISBN, hardback: 978-1-80227-208-6

This book is typeset in Droid Serif

For Clare and Alice

Contents

VIII

Preface

I was a senior manager running a large nuclear plant when I first realised I needed to change. I had been in a meeting with a member of my independent oversight team called John. He presented a number of findings from a report into the loss of a Royal Air Force aircraft in Afghanistan which resulted in the deaths of all 14 crew members. I had read the summary reports into the accident and was clear in my mind that it was as a result of a fire and then an explosion. Although some of the summaries mentioned leadership and management failings, the presentation given by John was truly frightening. He articulated so many missed opportunities and mistakes that I was not aware of, having read only the event summaries.

As a result of this presentation, I decided to read the full report. While reading the report "THE NIMROD REVIEW An independent review into the broader issues surrounding the loss of the RAF Nimrod MR2 Aircraft XV230 in Afghanistan in 2006", I was gripped by the descriptions of the actions taken by the senior managers and leaders involved. That led me to read about several other accidents and disasters. I spent months reading formal reports and found myself going on a journey of thought. Initially, I couldn't believe how blind these leaders had been to the obvious error of their ways. They had failed to lead and were complacent, overconfident and arrogant. How could they fail in so many simple ways? The basics were being missed time and again.

But as I read, my thoughts began to change. I started seeing more and more of the "failings" as credible in my own business and in others I had worked with or in. The more I read, the more I saw. I became aware of behaviours that I had not recognised in the past, although on reflection, they had always been there. For example, I saw that the tendency of leaders to emphasise the human error or personal choice aspects of investigations was commonplace. The systemic failures, for which the leaders were responsible, received little attention. This behaviour was not the preserve of "draconian" or "macho" organisations; it existed in businesses which professed to have "no-blame" or "just" cultures. I also noted that leaders who claimed to be very well-versed in the causes of these accidents displayed the very behaviours that I believed were at their core.

The people mentioned in these reports were not some distant, rare group who had been struck down with a savage case of incompetence. The behaviours they exhibited were not unique to their special case of ineptitude. They were, in fact, very common, and I had unconsciously behaved in many of the same ways at numerous points in my career. The difference was that they didn't get away with it. That realisation terrified me.

I set off with a clear purpose: I was not going to be a name in one of these reports. I would learn as much as I could and put in place things to prevent me from making the same mistakes.

I had watched television documentaries and read the summaries of these accidents. They all focused on the immediate "violation" by the individual(s) at the moment that the bad thing happened. It was only when I read the reports in full that I realised that the cause of these accidents was clearly rooted in management and leadership. Yes, a person fell asleep; yes, a pickup truck was in the wrong place; yes, an operator became distracted, but these things were the final act in a long chain of events. I would imagine that most people would argue that, in normal life, these simple acts or omissions should not inexorably lead to fatalities. One would hope that there were many other barriers between life and death.

This book is not intended to give solutions to the problems that I highlight; nor will it detail all of the problems that existed in each of the events. I have chosen those that resonated with me as a senior leader in a high-hazard industry. I hope that it will, at the very least, cause you to pause and look at yourself and the way you run your business to make sure that you are not making the same mistakes.

Chapter 1
Incident Summaries

In this short chapter, I will outline the basics of each of the events considered in this book.

Piper Alpha

On the 6th of July 1988, an oil platform in the North Sea owned by Occidental suffered fires and explosions which killed 167 men. The cause of the explosion is thought to have been a leak from a temporary blanking plate which had been fitted to a pump that was out of service for maintenance. A Permit to Work (PTW) process was in place on the platform. This process should have ensured that the pump was isolated correctly to remove all foreseeable hazards and should have highlighted to the workers on the rig that the pump was not to be used.

On this occasion, there were two separate PTWs open on the same pump. One of the permits was to remove a valve for testing, requiring a temporary blanking plate to be fitted in its place. It appears that the presence of two permits was not known to some of the workers on the rig as when the "duty" pump failed, they removed the electrical isolations on the pump that was out of service for maintenance and attempted to run it. As the pump ran, flammable material leaked from the blanking plate and came into contact with an ignition source.

The explosions and fires damaged the oil and gas lines which connected Piper Alpha to a network of pipes on the sea floor which was shared by several rigs. Unfortunately, other rigs in the network continued pumping oil and gas for some time, despite knowing that Piper Alpha was in distress. Although this contributed to the severity of the incident, the failure of the pipes is likely to have been catastrophic even if they had shut down earlier. The pipes would still have contained a significant volume of pressurised flammable material as the depressurisation procedure took hours to execute.

Nimrod XV230

Nimrod was an aircraft used by the Royal Air Force (RAF) for patrol, strike and reconnaissance duties. Having entered operational service in 1969, by the time of its loss in 2006, XV230 was an ageing airframe.

XV230 was on patrol over Afghanistan with a crew of 14. It had completed an air-to-air refuelling operation when fire broke out. The crew descended rapidly and attempted to return to base. Unfortunately, the aircraft exploded before they were able to reach safety and all on board were killed. The cause of the fire is believed to have been a fuel leak which led to highly flammable aviation fuel encountering a piece of equipment that was at high temperature.

King's Cross

On a winter evening in 1987, King's Cross underground station in London was the scene of a fatal fire. The fire, which killed 31 people, is believed to have been started when a smoker discarded a lit match. The match fell onto the running tracks of an escalator and ignited the grease and detritus under the treads. Having been observed and reported to staff, the fire was initially considered small and manageable. It would, however, suddenly grow and produce a large amount of flame which moved rapidly up the escalator and into the ticket hall.

Herald of Free Enterprise

Herald of Free Enterprise was a roll-on/roll-off vehicle and passenger ferry. Having operated a route between Dover and Calais, the Herald of Free Enterprise was redeployed to a route between Dover and Zeebrugge. In 1987, shortly after departing the port of Zeebrugge, the ship capsized, killing 193 people. This death toll could have been higher had the ship not come to rest on her side in shallow water, as opposed to inverting completely in deeper water.

When rescuers reached the ship, they found that the bow doors were open, exposing the car deck to the sea. The person who should have shut the doors had fallen asleep.

Imperial Sugar

Imperial Sugar owned a refinery in Georgia, USA, which had been built in 1916. In February 2008, a sugar dust explosion killed 14 people. The machinery and practices had degraded, leading to widespread accumulations of sugar.

Texas City Refinery

In 2005 an explosion occurred at the BP Texas City oil refinery, killing 15 people. The explosion occurred when flammable hydrocarbons were released from a process unit. The hydrocarbons are thought to have been ignited by the engine of an unattended truck.

Three Mile Island

In 1979 a partial meltdown occurred at the Three Mile Island nuclear power plant in Pennsylvania. The accident resulted in a release of activity from the facility and significant damage to the reputation of nuclear power generation in the USA. The ultimate cause of the partial meltdown was a loss of coolant caused by a pressure relief valve that stuck open. The operators were misled by the control room instrumentation and did not realise that the valve was open because the indicator light showed that it was shut. The light did not actually indicate the position of the valve itself; instead, it indicated the status of a solenoid that was associated with the valve.

Airgas Florida

In the summer of 2016, an explosion occurred at an Airgas manufacturing facility in Florida. The explosion is thought to have been caused when, during an operation to pump a chemical called nitrous oxide, the chemical was inadvertently heated above its safe temperature. This caused a dangerous reaction in the pump, which spread to the trailer that was being loaded, causing the trailer to explode. One worker was killed in the incident.

DuPont La Porte

In late 2014, 4 people were killed at the DuPont La Porte chemical facility. A significant quantity of the highly toxic chemical methyl mercaptan was released inside an insecticide production facility. This release resulted in death by asphyxiation and acute exposure to the chemical.

Columbia

In early 2003, 7 NASA astronauts were killed when their shuttle disintegrated on re-entry to the earth's atmosphere. Space shuttle Columbia had been damaged on launch when a piece of foam detached from a fuel tank and struck the leading edge of the left wing. The foam punched a hole in the heat shield of the wing. On re-entry, hot gases entered the wing and caused catastrophic damage to the wing structure. As the wing failed, control was lost and the shuttle disintegrated.

Deepwater Horizon

11 workers were killed in April 2010 when the Deepwater Horizon rig suffered a blowout (an uncontrolled release of flammable material) and explosion in the Gulf of Mexico. The accident also resulted in a large oil spill and significant environmental damage as the well was not capped for months.

Chapter 2
Are You Sure?

In this chapter, we will focus on the consequences of failing to risk assess business decisions. This includes the unintended consequences of seemingly simple changes, cost-cutting and extending the life of facilities and assets.

Unintended Consequences

Some business decisions bring risks. Most of the time, those risks are remote and small. There are, however, times when risks are significant and high consequence. These are not always obvious, particularly when they arise as a result of a number of seemingly discrete, unrelated decisions taken over an extended period of time.

In many industries, the concept of "risk assessment" is well known and practised on a daily basis on the "shop floor". Activities that could expose people to risk are often rigorously assessed, and a "hierarchy of controls" is applied to prevent injury. What is less common is the application of risk assessment to business decisions. In comparison to the activities carried out by those at the "coal face", business decisions made at senior levels can result in much more significant harm or hurt, yet they are not always assessed to determine what the outcomes may be. They are made in board rooms, frequently with little or no challenge. In the case of the Herald of Free Enterprise, a seemingly simple instruction to sail 15 minutes early as standard practice contributed greatly to the disaster. The order illustrates the apparent lack of thought given by management to the organisation of the officers' duties.

The sense of urgency to sail at the earliest possible moment was exemplified by an internal memorandum sent to assistant managers by <u>Mr. D. Shipley</u>, who was the operations manager at Zeebrugge. It is dated 18th August 1986 and the relevant parts of it read as follows:

"There seems to be a general tendency of satisfaction if the ship has sailed two or three minutes early. Where a full load is present, then every effort has to be made to sail the ship 15 minutes earlier . . . . . I expect to read from now onwards, especially where FE8[1] is concerned, that the ship left 15 minutes early . . . . . put pressure on the first officer if you don't think he is moving fast enough. Have your load ready when the vessel is in and marshal your staff and machines to work efficiently. Let's put the record straight, sailing late out of Zeebrugge isn't on. It's 15 minutes early for us." Mr. A. P. Young sought to explain away that memorandum on the basis that the language was used merely for purposes of what he called <u>"motivation"</u>. But it was entirely in keeping with his own thouWghts at that time. On the 13th August 1986 Captain Thorne, the Senior Master of *FREE ENTERPRISE VIII*, sent a memorandum to Deck Officers with a copy to Mr. Young, in which he said:-

"Finally, one of the reasons for such late arrivals is due to late departures from Dover the cause of which is rarely due to any inefficiency on the port of Dover staff - just lack of time available to handle both discharge and loading together with storing (often only 30-40

---

1 [another vessel in the fleet called Free Enterprise 8]

minutes). This situation can often be assisted by an early sailing from Zeebrugge the previous voyage: Zeebrugge staff MUST be made aware of such necessity immediately upon arrival." Mr. Young replied:

"I would just like to state that I thoroughly endorse your action." The Court was left in no doubt that deck officers felt that there was no time to be wasted. The Company sought to say that this disaster could have been avoided if the Chief Officer had waited on G deck another three minutes. That is true. But the Company took no proper steps to ensure that the Chief Officer remained on G deck until the bow doors were closed. On the 6th March they were running late. The Herald sailed 5 minutes late. This may have contributed to Mr. Sabel's decision to leave G deck before the arrival of Mr. Stanley[2], which he anticipated.[3]

This could be put down to a simple case of "production pressure", but I believe that in doing so, we miss the real problem. I believe the issue is a lack of consideration for the unintended consequences of imposing the demand that the ship sail 15 minutes early. There appears to have been no consideration of whether this could be achieved safely and what needed to be put in place to enable the demand to be met without compromising safety. It is entirely possible that there was an assumption that the demand could be achieved safely without any form of assessment to support that belief. It appears to have been treated as a "business as usual" decision and so required no further thought.

A similar failure to recognise that there was a departure from normal operations occurred on Piper

---

2 [the Assistant Bosun who was responsible for shutting the bow doors but fell asleep]
3 HERALD OF FREE ENTERPRISE Report of Court No. 8074 Page 11.

Alpha. A substantial package of work was initiated while continuing operations. This, to me, represents a significant departure from normal operations and required careful consideration.

The decision to continue production on Piper and at the prevailing rate while carrying out a substantial and diverse programme of construction and maintenance works is puzzling. If this course was to be followed, it should have required strengthened management and supervision on the platform. In event 2 senior posts, lead safety operator and deputy maintenance superintendent, were vacant and 3 posts, maintenance superintendent, operations superintended and deputy operations superintendent, were filled by personnel who had been temporarily upgraded. The abnormal mode of operation and any upset conditions should have put platform management on the alert for any sign of impending problems. In the event on the evening of the disaster any decision as to whether to shut down production was left to the judgement of the lead production operator. He would have learnt how to cope with such a decision by an experienced lead operator working with him initially "to show him the ropes". There were no exercises or scenarios to give practice in dealing with this type of situation. Usually there was no time for him to refer the question of a partial or total shutdown to the OIM[4]. Invariably he would have to make the decision himself and he would inform not the OIM but the operations superintendent first. At least in the unusual conditions in which the platform was being operated prior to the disaster this seems to me to have imposed an excessive burden on the lead production

4 [Offshore Installation Manager – the person on board the rig in overall charge]

operator and compounded the risk of something going wrong. I find it surprising that management did not consider that it was their responsibility to provide the lead production operator with greater support or guidance for this period during which process upsets were more likely and could call for the shutting down of production.[5]

It can be difficult to recognise when we move from normal operations into a special or abnormal condition that requires special assessment. It is made much more challenging when the culture of an organisation does not encourage a questioning attitude and "healthy unease" regarding safety. Developing such a culture takes a significant amount of time and effort.

As described by Exxon-Mobil CEO Rex Tillerson in response to questions before the National Commission, an organization's safety culture takes time (several decades) to develop and has to be grown from within—you can't buy or import a recipe—it has to be nurtured from within the organization. Exxon-Mobil has been at it now for more than twenty years, after learning the hard way and paying for its complacency and risk management failures that led to the Valdez spill. Since that time, Exxon-Mobil has introduced many positive innovations to improve safety culture, such as their Operations Integrity Management System (OIMS), introduced in 1992 as an integral part of their overall safety management system.

In contrast, at the time of the Macondo blowout[6], BP's corporate culture remained one that was embedded in

---

5 The Public Inquiry Into the Piper Alpha Disaster Volume 1 Page 235.
6 [the Deepwater Horizon incident]

risk-taking and cost-cutting – much like was found to be its case in 2005 (Texas City), in 2006 (Alaska North Slope Spill), and in 2010 ("The Spill"). Whether or not there is "evidence" that someone in the Macondo well project made a conscious decision to put costs before safety misses the more important point. It is the underlying safety culture, much of it so ingrained as to be unconscious, that governs the actions of an organization and its personnel. Cultural influences that permeate an organization and an industry and manifest in actions that can either promote and nurture a high reliability organization with high reliability systems, or actions reflective of complacency, excessive risk-taking, and a loss of team situational awareness. [7]

Cost-Cutting

A key contributor to a number of the accidents covered in this book is cost-cutting. There is a big difference between cuts and efficiencies. Cuts can leave a "hole" in an organisation, while genuine efficiencies create the balance between safety, quality, delivery and cost (SQDC). When cuts are made, services, safety barriers and "defence in depth" can be degraded. It is easy to fall into the trap of believing that we do not need as many safety barriers as we have because we have not had an accident for years. It may, however, be that we have not had an accident because of the number of safety barriers we have. A risk assessment is required.

In the case of Nimrod, the cost-cutting activities were branded in many different ways over a number of years.

---

7 Final Report on the Investigation of the Macondo Well Blowout Deepwater Horizon Study Group March 1, 2011 Page 87.

Financial pressures (in the shape of "cuts", "savings", "efficiencies", "strategic targets", "reduction in output costs", "leaning", etc.) drove a cascade of multifarious organisational changes (called variously "change", "initiatives", "change initiatives", "transformation", "re-energising", etc.) which led to a dilution of the airworthiness regime and culture within the MOD[8] and distraction from safety and airworthiness issues. There was a shift in culture and priorities in the MOD toward "business" and financial targets, at the expense of functional values such as safety and airworthiness. The Defence Logistics Organisation, in particular, came under huge pressure. Its primary focus became delivering "change" and the "change programme" and achieving the "Strategic Goal" of a 20% reduction in output costs in five years and other financial savings.[9]

The figure of 20 percent was not assessed for deliverability or potential impact.

In Texas City, a similar series of cuts were made despite falling facility performance.

The BP Chief Executive and the BP Board of Directors did not exercise effective safety oversight. Decisions to cut budgets were made at the highest levels of the BP Group despite serious safety deficiencies at Texas City. BP executives directed Texas City to cut capital expenditures in the 2005 budget by an additional 25 percent despite three major accidents and fatalities at the refinery in 2004.[10]

---

8 [Ministry of Defence]
9 The Nimrod Review Page 355.
10 U.S. CHEMICAL SAFETY AND HAZARD INVESTIGATION BOARD INVESTIGATION REPORT. REPORT NO. 2005-04-I-TX REFINERY EXPLOSION AND FIRE TEXAS CITY, TEXAS MARCH 23, 2005 Page 189.

Executives can behave in a way that is almost schizophrenic. They preach about deteriorating safety performance and insist that those below improve, thus implying blame, then cut operating budgets while safety and plant performance are degrading.

Capital spending was <u>reduced 84 percent</u> from 1992 to 2000. The analysis found "a consistent and significant reduction" in fixed costs at the refinery between 1992 and 1999, when fixed costs were reduced 52 percent, and the report highlighted a 25 percent budget cut targeted in 1999-2000 in the wake of the BP and Amoco merger. During the same period in the 1990s, total maintenance spending was reduced 41 percent.[11]

Year-on-year cuts can go unnoticed, and the impact of these cuts on safety is not realised until it is too late. A 10 percent cut is made one year, and when the first day of the new financial year arrives, we press the reset button. This appears to wipe the memory of all involved, and we apply another 10 percent cut in the new financial year. The cycle continues year after year and conditions deteriorate. We are lucky if we notice before a significant event occurs and we are able to take preventative action. Those in this chapter were not so fortunate.

This lack of consideration or awareness of the potential consequences of cost-cutting was evident in the behaviour of NASA's administrator, Daniel Goldin.

Goldin described himself as "sharp-edged" and could often be blunt. He rejected the criticism that he was sacrificing safety in the name of efficiency. In 1994 he told an audience at the Jet Propulsion Laboratory,

11 U.S. CHEMICAL SAFETY AND HAZARD INVESTIGATION BOARD INVESTIGATION RE-PORT. REPORT NO. 2005-04-I-TX REFINERY EXPLOSION AND FIRE TEXAS CITY, TEXAS MARCH 23, 2005 Page 157.

"When I ask for the budget to be cut, I'm told it's going to impact safety on the Space Shuttle . . . I think that's a bunch of crap."[12]

This statement clearly set the tone; it is likely that people would feel that they were unable to challenge the decision to cut budgets given the language used by Goldin. Cuts were clearly very important to him, and it is possible that in order to please the boss or avoid negative consequences, people would make decisions and/or take actions that would be questionable in normal circumstances.

A drive for efficiency is absolutely the correct thing to do. However, it needs to be planned and monitored. If it is not, it can take on a life of its own and rage out of control.

> Workforce reductions instituted by Administrator Goldin as he attempted to redefine the agency's mission and its overall organization also added to the turbulence of his reign. In the 1990s, the overall NASA workforce was reduced by 25 percent through normal attrition, early retirements, and buyouts—cash bonuses for leaving NASA employment. NASA operated under a hiring freeze for most of the decade, making it difficult to bring in new or younger people.[13]

Recruitment freezes can damage the business. A "black hole" moves through the organisation over the years. This hole means that there is a lack of knowledge, experience and talent in a generation, or multiple generations, of the workforce.

> NASA Headquarters was particularly affected by workforce reductions. More than half its employees left or were transferred in parallel with the 1996 transfer of

---

12 Columbia Accident Investigation Board Page 106.
13 Columbia Accident Investigation Board Page 110.

program management responsibilities back to the NASA centers. The Space Shuttle Program bore more than its share of Headquarters personnel cuts. Headquarters civil service staff working on the Space Shuttle Program went from 120 in 1993 to 12 in 2003.

While the overall workforce at the NASA Centers involved in human space flight was not as radically reduced, the combination of the general workforce reduction and the introduction of the Space Flight Operations Contract significantly impacted the Centers' Space Shuttle Program civil service staff. Johnson Space Center went from 1,330 in 1993 to 738 in 2002; Marshall Space Flight Center, from 874 to 337; and Kennedy Space Center from 1,373 to 615. Kennedy Director Roy Bridges argued that personnel cuts were too deep, and threatened to resign unless the downsizing of his civil service workforce, particularly those involved with safety issues, was reversed.

By the end of the decade, NASA realized that staff reductions had gone too far. By early 2000, internal and external studies convinced NASA leaders that the workforce needed to be revitalized. These studies noted that "five years of buyouts and downsizing have led to serious skill imbalances and an overtaxed core workforce. As more employees have departed, the workload and stress [on those] remaining have increased, with a corresponding increase in the potential for impacts to operational capacity and safety." NASA announced that NASA workforce downsizing would stop short of the 17,500 target, and that its human space flight centers would immediately hire several hundred workers.[14]

---

14 Columbia Accident Investigation Board Page 110.

Using attrition as a means of reducing the workforce can be very effective. However, it should be closely monitored as it is an indiscriminate tool. The outcomes that NASA experienced were foreseeable. Had they "black-hatted" or critically assessed the proposals, they could have seen these as potential issues and mitigated them.

This conviction that an organisation is "flabby" and inefficient may well be true, but it does not mean that consideration should not be given to the potential negative outcomes of a drive to cut costs. A belief "without study" that the business can absorb the reductions can be dangerous. This appears to have been the case in the Nimrod incident.

The DLO's[15] allocation was some 20%, or approximately £4.6 billion, of the total MOD budget. The subsequent years' allocations were, however, subject to two further financial reductions imposed by the SDR[16]: (a) a 3% cut in the total budget; and (b) 3% assumed annual efficiency savings, as explained below. In 2000, the MOD began to move from cash-based financial management to RAB[17]. The burden of implementing this change "fell particularly heavily on all staff across the DLO". During Sir Sam Cowan's time as CDL[18], however, financial accounting in-year continued to be run on a cash basis, i.e. at the start of each year he was given a cash allocation which he could not exceed.

Thus, all budget reductions were [to] be made at source, i.e. it was assumed at the beginning of the financial year that the targets for reductions in output costs and annual efficiency savings would be met and funds were

---

15 [Defence Logistics Organisation]
16 [Strategic Defence Review]
17 [Resource Accounting and Budgeting]
18 [Chief of Defence Logistics]

deducted from the budget funds allocated for each financial year accordingly. It followed that each service or organisation faced a shortfall at the end of the financial year if the targeted savings were not made. The iron rule was the services had to live within the cash provided. The cash was being taken before the savings were in fact delivered.[19]

The assumption that the reduction can be made means that budgets are cut at the start of the financial year. This is before any work to reduce costs has been done and means that costs are cut whether or not it is safe to do so. Your people are behind the curve from the outset, and they will scrabble around trying to meet the demand to cut while trying to deliver the "day job". In the case of NASA, an apparent belief that the reductions were safe and achievable, without actually assessing them, led to unfounded optimism.

Faced with this budget situation, NASA had the choice of either eliminating major programs or achieving greater efficiencies while maintaining its existing agenda. Agency leaders chose to attempt the latter. They continued to develop the space station, continued robotic planetary and scientific missions, and continued Shuttle-based missions for both scientific and symbolic purposes. In 1994 they took on the responsibility for developing an advanced technology launch vehicle in partnership with the private sector. They tried to do this by becoming more efficient. "Faster, better, cheaper" became the NASA slogan of the 1990s.[20]

The same can be seen in Texas City. But in this case, one

---

19 The Nimrod Review Pages 371 and 372.
20 Columbia Accident Investigation Board Page 103.

business unit leader realised the danger and chose not to follow the instructions of his superiors. His colleague, unfortunately, sought to carry out the instruction.

In 1999, the BP Group Chief Executive of R&M told the refining executive committee about the 25 percent cut and said that the target was a directive more than a loose target. One refinery Business Unit Leader considered the 25 percent reduction to be unsafe because it came on top of years of budget cuts in the 1990s; he refused to fully implement the target.[21]

There are two sides to cost-cutting: there is the cut of funding and then the acceptance of the cut without a commensurate reduction in scope. When a cut is imposed from "on high", if it goes wrong, we are as guilty as those who imposed it if we simply accept the cut without challenge or risk assessment. When a cut in funding is imposed, a check against committed scope is required. Is what you have been asked to do achievable with the funding you have? If not and you try to achieve it anyway, you are potentially walking into danger, as those involved in Nimrod experienced.

There was a "conspiracy of optimism" in [the] 1990s. This had the knock-on effect of a growing gap between the PAO[22] budgets and the actual cost of delivering logistics support two or three years down the line. A cash-based accounting system made the under-estimation of future resource costs possible. This was going to be less easy with RAB[23].

---

21 U.S. CHEMICAL SAFETY AND HAZARD INVESTIGATION BOARD INVESTIGATION RE-PORT. REPORT NO. 2005-04-I-TX REFINERY EXPLOSION AND FIRE TEXAS CITY, TEXAS MARCH 23, 2005 Page 159.
22 [Principal Administrative Officers]
23 [Resource Accounting and Budgeting]

13.51 On 1 April 2000, a six-page Corporate Plan was distributed to each of the 43,000 people working in the DLO[24] which announced the (so-called) "Strategic Goal" of a 20% reduction in output costs by 2005: "We are committing ourselves to a bold target. We will reduce our output costs by 20% by 2005 whilst ensuring that we continue to deliver and, indeed where appropriate, improve the quality of our outputs."

13.52.1 A "transformation" was required: "Quite simply, we have to achieve a transformation in how we deliver effective logistics support to the front line at a sustainable cost. This means that we must reduce the cost of our outputs, not by crude cuts but by changing the way we work."[25]

The desire to change the way we work is all well and good, but it is easy to make an assumption that we can or that we know how to change. If the change is not closely supported by senior leaders who provide clear expectations to drive that change, people may not change the way they work; they may simply cut costs.

Leaders create culture. It is their responsibility to change it. Top administrators must take responsibility for risk, failure, and safety by remaining alert to the effects their decisions have on the system. Leaders are responsible for establishing the conditions that lead to their subordinates' successes or failures.[26]

When faced with top-down pressure to reduce costs but maintain or increase operational tempo, there are only so many options available to the frontline leader. Headcount, quality of consumables, stocks of consumables and spares,

---

24 [Defence Logistics Organisation]
25 The Nimrod Review Pages 368 and 369.
26 Columbia Accident Investigation Board Page 203.

and maintenance/asset care budgets are easy targets. In general, raiding these areas will be fine in the short term, but they will yield unfavourable results in the medium to long term.

With Center infrastructure off-limits, this left the Space Shuttle budget as an obvious target for cuts. Because the Shuttle required a large "standing army" to keep it flying, reducing the size of the Shuttle workforce became the primary means by which top leaders lowered the Shuttle's operating costs. These personnel reduction efforts started early in the decade and continued through most of the 1990s. They created substantial uncertainty and tension within the Shuttle workforce, as well as the transitional difficulties inherent in any large-scale workforce reassignment.[27]

Although not explicitly noted as cost-cutting in the official report, it appears that a similar effect was experienced in the Imperial Sugar incident. The poor material condition of the facility, which had caused a series of "near misses" associated with sugar dust and the well-documented hazard of fire and explosion, suggests a lack of investment.

Workers told CSB[28] investigators that sugar spillage and dust generation were constant problems in the packing buildings. They reported that sugar leaked from worn seals, loose or missing covers, and other breaches in the aging screw conveyors, bucket elevators, hoppers, and other bulk sugar transport devices. Leaks in the pressurized air ducts used to transport cornstarch, and the occasional powdered sugar packaging machine malfunction, released dust into the work areas. In addition, sugar-filled paper or plastic containers

27 Columbia Accident Investigation Board Page 106.
28 [U.S. Chemical Safety and Hazard Investigation Board]

sometimes tore open and spilled their contents as they traveled along the conveyors,[33] generating more sugar dust. However, because the large work areas were typically not equipped with dust removal systems, the dust released from these sources would float in the air and settle on overhead piping, equipment, lights, ceiling support beams, and any other horizontal surface.

Packaging machines required frequent cleaning to operate properly. Workers routinely used water or steam, and sometimes industrial vacuum cleaners to remove sugar and sugar dust from equipment and work areas. But they also routinely used compressed air to remove accumulated granulated sugar or sugar dust from packaging equipment. Compressed air cleaning only lofted dust into the air where it would later accumulate on horizontal surfaces in the area. More frequent cleaning was needed to remove dust in the work areas, especially on elevated surfaces, before it accumulated to hazardous levels, but was not routinely performed.

Because Imperial Sugar manufactured and packaged food-grade sugar products, general area cleanliness (removal of trash and other debris) was necessary to prevent product contamination and control rodents. Spilled sugar also presented a slip or trip hazard, especially when wet, as workers reported was often the case throughout the facility.

Written housekeeping policies included planned daily, weekly, and monthly packaging area cleaning schedules, but workers reported that these policies were not effectively implemented. Pre-incident photographs of equipment and packaging areas, worker injury reports in 2006 and 2007, and a December 2007 quality assurance survey provided evidence that the housekeeping practices were inadequate—deep piles of spilled granulated and powdered sugar accumulated around and on equipment, and sugar dust accumulated on floors, equipment, and other elevated horizontal surfaces. Workers interviewed by the CSB investigators reported cleaning activities were seldom performed on hard-to-reach elevated surfaces and some powdered sugar packaging areas frequently had dense sugar dust in the air.[29]

Workers told the CSB investigators that occasionally, small fires occurred in the packing buildings when sugar or packaging material was ignited by a hot electrical device or overheated bearing. As recently as January 2008, one worker observed flames "3 feet high" before he and other workers in the area extinguished the fire with portable fire extinguishers. As noted in Section 3.6.3, the explosion panels on a dust collector were blown open when the dust inside the collector was ignited. None of these events resulted in a widespread fire or secondary dust explosion. Fires and even dust explosions occurred at the Imperial Sugar facilities and other sugar refineries without ever propagating into a secondary dust explosion or large fire. The unsafe work practices continued and the combustible dust hazards were not abated.

The CSB concluded that the small events and near-misses caused company management, and the managers and workers at both the Port Wentworth, Georgia, and Gramercy, Louisiana, facilities to lose sight of the

29 INVESTIGATION REPORT. Report No. 2008-05-I-GA September 2009 SUGAR DUST EXPLOSION AND FIRE Pages 45 and 46.

ongoing and significant hazards posed by accumulated sugar dust in the packing buildings. Imperial Sugar management and staff accepted a riskier condition and failed to correct the ongoing hazardous conditions, despite the well-known and broadly published hazards associated with combustible sugar dust accumulation in the workplace.[30]

A lack of investment in maintaining facility standards, the material condition of equipment and supporting services was also at the heart of the events in Texas City.

While some BP refinery leaders resisted the call for a 25 percent reduction in fixed costs, Texas City made serious cuts and came close to the 25 percent reduction target. Its cost reduction strategy was to "aggressively drive costs out of the system at an accelerated pace relative to other refiners." The strategy indicated that the cuts would be accomplished through destaffing, outsourcing, and eliminating unnecessary turnaround costs. Items cut included turnarounds; safety committee meetings; the central training organization; fire drills; maintenance, engineering, supervision, and inspection staff; plant maintenance; and training courses. Safety and maintenance expenditures were a significant portion of the cuts. The refinery's capital expenditures to maintain safe plant operation and to comply with HSE[31] legal requirements were cut $33 million, or 45 percent, from 1998 to 1999.[32]

The impact of cost-cutting can be further amplified by

---

30 INVESTIGATION REPORT. Report No. 2008-05-I-GA September 2009 SUGAR DUST EXPLOSION AND FIRE Page 49.
31 [Health and Safety Executive]
32 U.S. CHEMICAL SAFETY AND HAZARD INVESTIGATION BOARD INVESTIGATION REPORT. REPORT NO. 2005-04-I-TX REFINERY EXPLOSION AND FIRE TEXAS CITY, TEXAS MARCH 23, 2005 Page 159.

increases in operational tempo. An ageing asset which has not been adequately invested in is expected to perform at a higher rate. This can be compounded by other issues which combine to degrade safety performance. When an organisation has been through year-on-year cost cuts, reductions in the number of people available, increasing obsolescence of key equipment and the degradation of assets, the likelihood of suffering a significant incident grows tremendously.

This budget squeeze also came at a time when the Space Shuttle Program exhibited a trait common to most ageing systems: increased costs due to greater maintenance requirements, a declining second- and third-tier contractor support base, and deteriorating infrastructure. Maintaining the Shuttle was becoming more expensive at a time when Shuttle budgets were decreasing or being held constant. Only in the last few years have those budgets begun a gradual increase. [33]

This is the same as the Nimrod incident. The asset was ageing and the operational tempo was increasing while costs were being cut. In the case of Texas City, the operational performance of the facility was degrading year on year, and production pressure continued to grow.

In the July 2004 presentation, Texas City managers also spoke to the ongoing need to address the site's reliability and mechanical integrity issues and financial pressures. The presentation suggested that a number of unplanned events in the process units led to the refinery being behind target for reliability, citing the UU4[34] fire and other outages and shutdowns. The presentation stated that "poorly directed historic investment and

33 Columbia Accident Investigation Board Page 105.
34 [Ultraformer Unit #4]

costly configuration yield middle of the pack returns." The conclusion was that Texas City was not returning a profit commensurate with its needs for capital, despite record profits at the refinery. The presentation indicated that a new 1,000-day goal had been added to reduce maintenance expenditures to "close the 25 percent gap in maintenance spending" identified from Solomon benchmarking.[35]

In the face of an unreliable plant and several accidents, the maintenance budget was cut, thus reducing the maintenance performed and making the plant less reliable. This was the power of target fixation!

Asset Life Extensions

When a facility or asset is required to operate for a specific period of time, people will make decisions about investment, asset care (maintaining and renewing equipment) and the ability to "live with" sub-optimal conditions based on the time the facility has to run. They may choose to cancel projects that will not be delivered in sufficient time to make a difference. They may choose to operate a maintenance regime that is "run to failure", as opposed to proactive interventions to prolong the life of the equipment. These decisions can be valid, depending on the asset life conditions faced by the decision-makers. It is important that when we choose to extend the life of an asset, we have in mind the many decisions which will have been made over the years assuming the original lifespan. These decisions may mean that the facility we intend to extend the life of is not in the condition we would expect. We may have:

---

35 U.S. CHEMICAL SAFETY AND HAZARD INVESTIGATION BOARD INVESTIGATION RE-PORT. REPORT NO. 2005-04-I-TX REFINERY EXPLOSION AND FIRE TEXAS CITY, TEXAS MARCH 23, 2005 Page 169.

- Stopped maintaining it
- Stopped recruitment
- Reduced training capability
- Worked around problems as "it isn't for very long, we will get by"
- Reduced funding

All of these things can be tolerated for a short time but will need to be addressed when we extend the life of the asset. This is particularly problematic when there is asset life "creep". As opposed to a single decision to extend the life by X years, a series of small extensions are made. Phrases like "sweat the asset" creep into management speak, and the problems associated with each small extension are compounded by the next.

The Shuttle was mischaracterised by the 1995 Kraft Report as "a mature and reliable system . . . about as safe as today's technology will provide." Based on this mischaracterization, NASA believed that it could turn increased responsibilities for Shuttle operations over to a single prime contractor and reduce its direct involvement in ensuring safe Shuttle operations, instead monitoring contractor performance from a more detached position. NASA also believed that it could use the "mature" Shuttle to carry out operational missions without continually focusing engineering attention on understanding the mission-by-mission anomalies inherent in a developmental vehicle.

In the 1990s, the planned date for replacing the Shuttle shifted from 2006 to 2012 and then to 2015 or later. Given the uncertainty regarding the Shuttle's service life, there has been policy and budgetary ambivalence on investing in the vehicle. Only in the past year has

NASA begun to provide the resources needed to sustain extended Shuttle operations. Previously, safety and support upgrades were delayed or deferred, and Shuttle infrastructure was allowed to deteriorate.[36]

King's Cross, NASA and Nimrod all experienced a similar "creep" of asset lifespan which resulted in a paralysis of investment. In the case of King's Cross, this creep led to the deferral of safety-significant projects.

The automatic operation of water fog equipment was envisaged as early as 1948. Essentially the problem was to find a detection system for smoke or heat which would cover the entire escalator system and be sufficiently sensitive to detect a fire early enough for the water fog to be able to extinguish it. An initial trial of smoke detection equipment on an escalator at Tottenham Court Road in 1954 was followed by a second stage in 1964 when equipment was installed on two escalators at Baker Street and a further two at Paddington. These did not automatically operate the water fog equipment but did incorporate an alarm system. Over the next ten years there were numerous proposals to install smoke detection equipment on other escalators, including the Northern Line and Piccadilly Line escalators at King's Cross. However, no action was taken because, on one occasion, the proposal was inadvertently left out of the budget, and subsequently the proposal was rejected on the grounds that the M series escalators did not have enough life left in them to justify the expenditure. It was also said that the detection equipment gave more false alarms than real ones. In fact some of the M series escalators were expected to remain in service into the

---

36 Columbia Accident Investigation Board Page 118.

next century.[37]

I am not suggesting that every business decision should be formally risk assessed. I am also not suggesting that a long, complex process be applied to those which are subject to risk assessment; a graded approach is more appropriate. The categories identified in this chapter (cost-cutting, asset life extensions, loss of soft services, reductions in maintenance, etc.) are those which have the potential to have significant consequences if not carefully considered. They are likely to be applicable in many industries, but there will be other categories which may be unique to specific circumstances and businesses. The assessment process should take into account what has come before. Decisions and changes may have been made which could move the business away from what is considered to be the baseline configuration and so invalidate our assumptions.

Twice in NASA history, the agency embarked on a slippery slope that resulted in catastrophe. Each decision, taken by itself, seemed correct, routine, and indeed, insignificant and unremarkable. Yet in retrospect, the cumulative effect was stunning.[38]

---

37 Investigation into the King's Cross Underground Fire King's Cross Page 45.
38 Columbia Accident Investigation Board Page 203.

Chapter 3
Someone Should Have Done Something About That

There are shortfalls and deficiencies in every business. Most are inconsequential; some, however, are not. Not resolving issues that are well known, often reported numerous times, or not completing safety actions recommended after audits or other oversight activities/investigations, is all too common. Operating with known defects without consciously risk assessing whether it is safe to do so is a potential road to ruin. These defects become normal over time; there is a drift away from safety, and a "normalisation of deviance" creeps in.

<u>Known Problems Not Resolved</u>

When known problems are not resolved and there is a requirement to keep operating, a formal assessment of the safety of that decision should be made. This may result in a decision not to operate based on safety concerns. When it results in a decision to operate, it enables additional safeguards to be put in place to compensate for the degraded condition.

It is relatively rare, in my experience, to have a significant event whose cause came as a complete surprise to all involved. More often than not, there is someone who says, "Yeah, we knew about that," or words to that effect. In the next chapter, I will cover some of the reasons people fail to address known problems in more detail.

Deviance is not restricted to the material condition of equipment or facilities. Leaders and managers often focus on procedural use and adherence when embarking on a human performance improvement programme. This focus rarely includes their own behaviour. In the case of Columbia, NASA management knowingly violated a key design specification aimed at ensuring the safety of the shuttle and its crew as a matter of routine.

> Despite the design requirement that the External Tank shed no debris, and that the Orbiter not be subjected to any significant debris hits, Columbia sustained damage from debris strikes on its inaugural 1981 flight. More than 300 tiles had to be replaced. Engineers stated that had they known in advance that the External Tank "was going to produce the debris shower that occurred" during launch, "they would have had a difficult time clearing Columbia for flight."

> Despite the high level of concern after STS-1[39] and through the Challenger accident, foam continued to separate from the External Tank. Photographic evidence of foam shedding exists for 65 of the 79 missions for which imagery is available.[40]

A similar situation existed in the Imperial Sugar incident. Again, a well-known safety issue was allowed to exist for a protracted period despite numerous fires.

> Imperial Sugar and the granulated sugar refining and packaging industry have been aware of sugar dust explosion hazards as far back as 1925.

> Port Wentworth facility management personnel were

39 [Space Transportation System – The flight or mission number]
40 Columbia Accident Investigation Board 122.

aware of sugar dust explosion hazards and emphasized the importance of properly designed dust handling equipment and good housekeeping practices to minimize dust accumulation as long ago as 1958, but did not take action to minimize and control sugar dust hazards.

"This dust problem has become so serious and dangerous in modern refineries . . . at present, we have so much to correct that is knowingly wrong, there is no need for outside help. We make a lot of dust in the plant and have had a very inefficient dust collecting system [;] consequently, it has been hopeless to try to keep the dry end of our plant clean. We have heavy accumulations of dust in several areas . . . we hope to improve the housekeeping around the silos." [41]

In the case of the Airgas explosion, there appears to have been no process in place to track known issues to resolution. Even the oversight function was not set up to ensure the resolution of issues; it focused instead on compliance with documents.

In this context, some responsibility for providing additional technical support could fall to the Airgas corporate safety function. The annual safety audit, however, conducted by a corporate Airgas safety official, lacked a process safety focus. This annual safety audit did not require her to delve into deeper aspects of the site's safety systems; rather, through a question and answer model, corporate practices required her to evaluate compliance with existing company policies. The Airgas audit program did not challenge the status quo with respect to existing, and in some cases long-

41 INVESTIGATION REPORT. Report No. 2008-05-I-GA September 2009 SUGAR DUST EXPLOSION AND FIRE Page 63.

standing, process safety issues.[42]

In a number of these accidents, exactly the same conditions had resulted in events that didn't have a significant negative outcome. This "free learning" or "near miss" could have prompted action. Unfortunately, in each case, it did not, and the next time the conditions appeared, there were disastrous consequences.

Statistics for fires on escalators between 1958 and 1987 were presented to the Investigation by London Underground. Records were held of over 400 fires and so-called smoulderings, some of which were serious enough to cause the evacuation of stations, serious delays, and considerable damage to the escalators involved. Until 1985 the only source of such statistics was the fire and fusing reports returned by station staff; the fuller record from station logs was available only from 1985. The position on the keeping and analysis of statistics on fires by London Underground was quite unsatisfactory.

Until 18 November 1987 there had been no fatalities as a result of escalator fires, although some people had suffered smoke inhalation, serious enough to be taken to hospital. The statistics indicate that 45% of these fires and smoulderings occurred on MH escalators, which were particularly prone to fires on their running tracks. The cause of these fires had usually been attributed to smokers' materials falling down between the treads and the skirting board and igniting the grease and detritus on the running track. That accumulation of dirt formed a seed bed for fire.

42 Nitrous Oxide Explosion - Airgas (Air Liquide) Cantonment, Florida August 28, 2016 - U.S. Chemical Safety and Hazard Investigation Board Investigation Report One Killed Report Number: 2016-04-I-FL Issue Date: February 2017 Pages 113 and 114.

A review of recent serious escalator fires and the Oxford Circus station fire, with the recommendations made in reports or by the internal inquiries into these fires, is given at Appendix J. The analysis shows that of the 46 serious escalator fires recorded over the last three decades, the cause of over two-thirds had been attributed to smokers' materials.[43]

They had already experienced an event or a disastrous set of circumstances on the same type of escalator, with the same ignition source, on multiple occasions but had not experienced the disastrous consequences.

The same situation existed in NASA prior to the loss of Columbia. It appears that the violation of the design specification became normal because the damage experienced had not been significant in the eyes of management. There was, however, an event that could have snapped them out of this mindset:

> One debris strike in particular foreshadows the STS-107[44] event. When Atlantis was launched on STS-27R on December 2, 1988, the largest debris event up to that time significantly damaged the Orbiter. Post-launch analysis of tracking camera imagery by the Intercenter Photo Working Group identified a large piece of debris that struck the Thermal Protection System tile at approximately 85 seconds into the flight. On Flight Day Two, Mission Control asked the flight crew to inspect Atlantis with a camera mounted on the remote manipulator arm, a robotic device that was not installed on Columbia for STS-107. Mission Commander R. L. "Hoot" Gibson later stated that Atlantis "looked like it had been blasted by a shotgun." Concerned that

43 Investigation into the King's Cross Underground Fire King's Cross Page 45.
44 [Space Transportation System – The flight or mission number]

the Orbiter's Thermal Protection System had been breached, Gibson ordered that the video be transferred to Mission Control so that NASA engineers could evaluate the damage.

When Atlantis landed, engineers were surprised by the extent of the damage. Post-mission inspections deemed it "the most severe of any mission yet flown." The Orbiter had 707 dings, 298 of which were greater than an inch in one dimension. Damage was concentrated outboard of a line right of the bipod attachment to the liquid oxygen umbilical line. Even more worrisome, the debris had knocked off a tile, exposing the Orbiter's skin to the heat of re-entry. Post-flight analysis concluded that structural damage was confined to the exposed cavity left by the missing tile, which happened to be at the location of a thick aluminum plate covering an L-band navigation antenna. Were it not for the thick aluminum plate, Gibson stated during a presentation to the Board, a burn-through may have occurred.[45]

Had NASA management acknowledged the potential consequences and acknowledged that, in all likelihood, luck alone had saved Atlantis, they could have taken steps to prevent a reoccurrence. In this case, the experience of failure became the memory of success, and the opportunity to learn from this near-disaster was missed. This was also the case in the Three Mile Island accident:

A senior engineer of the Babcock & Wilcox Company[46] (suppliers of the nuclear steam system) noted in an earlier accident, bearing strong similarities to the one at Three Mile Island, that operators had mistakenly turned

---

45 Columbia Accident Investigation Board Page 127.

46 [B&W]

off the emergency cooling system. He pointed out that we were lucky that the circumstances under which this error was committed did not lead to a serious accident and warned that under other circumstances (like those that would later exist at Three Mile Island), a very serious accident could result. He urged, in the strongest terms, that clear instructions be passed on to the operators. This memorandum was written 13 months before the accident at Three Mile Island, but no new instructions resulted from it. The Commission's investigation of this incident, and other similar incidents within B&W and the NRC[47], indicates that the lack of understanding that led the operators to incorrect action existed both within the Nuclear Regulatory Commission and within the utility and its suppliers.[48]

On this occasion, no meltdown occurred. In the case of Texas City, there were many indications that all was not well with the condition of the facility. Unlike the Atlantis experience, the consequences were significant:

Mechanical integrity problems previously identified in the 2002 study and the 2003 GHSER [Getting Health, Safety, and Environment Right] audit were warnings of the likelihood of a major accident. In March 2004, a furnace outlet pipe ruptured and resulted in fire that caused $30 million in damage. Texas City managers investigated and prepared an HRO[49] analysis of the accident to identify the underlying cultural issues. They found that in 2003 an inspector recommended examining the furnace outlet piping, but this was not done. Prior to the 2004 incident, thinning pipe

47 [Nuclear Regulatory Commission]
48 Report of the President's Commission on the accident at Three Mile Island Page 10.
49 [High Reliability Organization]

discovered in the outlet piping toward the end of a turnaround was not repaired, and, after the unit was started up, a hydrocarbon release from the thinning pipe caused a major fire. One key finding of the investigation was that "[w]e have created an environment where people 'justify putting off repairs to the future." The BP investigation team, which included the refinery maintenance manager and the West Plant Manufacturing Delivery Leader (MDL), also found an "intimidation to meet schedule and budget" when the discovery of the unsafe pipe conflicted with the schedule to start up UU4[50]. The team summarized its conclusions:

- "The incentives used in this workplace may encourage hiding mistakes."
- "We work under pressures that lead us to miss or ignore early indicators of potential problems."
- "Bad news is not encouraged."[51]

Despite this, no significant actions were taken to improve the overall condition of the facility. A lack of meaningful action in the face of repeat safety near misses also played a key role in the loss of the Herald of Free Enterprise.

before this disaster there had been no less than five occasions when one of the Company's ships had proceeded to sea with bow or stern doors open. Some of those incidents were known to the management, who had not drawn them to the attention of the other Masters.[52]

50 [Ultraformer Unit number 4]
51 U.S. CHEMICAL SAFETY AND HAZARD INVESTIGATION BOARD INVESTIGATION REPORT. REPORT NO. 2005-04-I-TX REFINERY EXPLOSION AND FIRE TEXAS CITY, TEXAS MARCH 23, 2005 Page 164.
52 HERALD OF FREE ENTERPRISE Report of Court No. 8074 Page 12.

The management team viewed the problem as a human failure (and so not their fault) as opposed to a system issue that required their attention. In the case of Nimrod XV230, the focus was equally misplaced.

A maintenance approach which relies primarily on a belief that all potential ignition sources have been eliminated is, in my view, unsound. Further, it is not generally a good approach to tolerate recurrent defects, even minor ones; they might have unexpected, unforeseen, or cumulative consequences. It is also a well-known adage that "fuel will tend to find a source of ignition". Liquid paths are eccentric. Accordingly, as I state in **chapter 23,** good practice, and the principle of As Low As Reasonably Practicable (ALARP), require that the risk of *both* parts of the ignition source/fuel sources equation be equally carefully addressed. One BOI[53] witness said that leaks "were seen more as an operational issue as opposed to a flight safety issue". It is right to point out, however, that if crew detect a fuel leak in flight they are expected to file an Incident Report (IR). Significant leaks on the ground would also be reported in an IR and probably supplemented by a Serious Fault Report (SFR). Ground crews are required to do all in their power to identify and cure a leak, and aircrew would not accept an aircraft to fly unless leaks were cured, or within limits and correctly recorded. Nonetheless, in the past, it appears that not enough was done to give thought to attempting to identify the underlying causes or patterns of leaks, or the potential risks flowing from them.[54]

A belief that leaks are inevitable led to efforts to prevent

53 [Board of Inquiry]
54 The Nimrod Review Page 84.

fires falling short. In King's Cross, a comparable "fatalistic" attitude existed. Fires were viewed as inevitable, and so preventative actions were not prioritised:

> Many of the shortcomings in the physical and human state of affairs at King's Cross on 18 November 1987 had in fact been identified before by the internal inquiries into escalator fires. They were also highlighted in reports by the fire brigade, police, and Railway Fire Prevention and Fire Safety Standards Committee. The many recommendations had not been adequately considered by senior managers and there was no way to ensure they were circulated, considered and acted upon. London Underground's failure to carry through the proposals resulting from earlier fires—such as the provision of automatic sprinklers, the need to ensure all fire equipment was correctly positioned and serviceable, identification of alternative means of escape, and the need to train staff to react properly and positively in emergencies was a failure which I believe contributed to the disaster at King's Cross.[55]

The information contained in the reports on fires had not reached those who would or could take action. The senior leaders had not implemented a system through which they could assure themselves that they would receive key information. They also appear to lack the desire to seek out information that would provide them with a complete picture of the state of their business. Occidental leaders also suffered from this apparent failure to be curious:

> The evidence which I have considered in this chapter should be considered along with my observations in Chapters 11–13. It appears to me that there

---

55 Investigation into the King's Cross Underground Fire King's Cross Page 117.

were significant flaws in the quality of Occidental's management of safety which affected the circumstances of the events of the disaster. Senior management were too easily satisfied that the PTW [Permit to Work] system was being operated correctly, relying on the absence of any feedback of problems as indicating that all was well. They failed to provide the training required to ensure that an effective PTW system was operated in practice. In the face of a known problem with the deluge system they did not become personally involved in probing the extent of the problem and what should be done to resolve it as soon as possible. They adopted a superficial response when issues of safety were raised by others, as for example at the time of Mr Saldana's report and the Sutherland prosecution. They failed to ensure that emergency training was being provided as they intended. Platform personnel and management were not prepared for a major emergency as they should have been.[56]

The senior leaders appear complacent and lack the drive to own long-standing issues with safety systems. When the deluge system (a large firefighting system) was significantly degraded and the rectification project was only a third complete after four years, they did not step in and prioritise the availability of the system.

This lack of a sense of personal accountability can be infectious. When senior leaders fail to demonstrate, through their own actions and behaviours, that safety is important, long-standing deviations creep in.

The chain further developed when the ineffective building ventilation system failed to be addressed after

---

56 The Public Inquiry Into the Piper Alpha Disaster Volume 1 Page 238.

DuPont auditors identified it as a safety concern about five years before the incident.[57]

These deviations often lead to a change in the working habits of those on the facilities. People can adjust the way tasks and operations are conducted to compensate for the deficiencies in equipment or facilities.

Management did not ensure that unit operational problems were corrected over time, leading operators to deviate from established procedures.[58]

When procedures are not updated or do not reflect actual practice, operators and supervisors learn not to rely on procedures for accurate instructions. Other major accident investigations reveal that workers frequently develop work practices to adjust to real conditions not addressed in the formal procedures. Human factors expert James Reason refers to these adjustments as "necessary violations," where departing from the procedures is necessary to get the job done (Hopkins, 2000). Management's failure to regularly update the procedures and correct operational problems encouraged this practice: "If there have been so many process changes since the written procedures were last updated that they are no longer correct, workers will create their own unofficial procedures that may not adequately address safety issues" (API 770, 2001).[59]

These "necessary violations" develop when issues are not resolved. In many cases, the workers stop reporting

57 Toxic Chemical Release at the DuPont La Porte Chemical Facility Page 8.
58 U.S. CHEMICAL SAFETY AND HAZARD INVESTIGATION BOARD INVESTIGATION RE-PORT. REPORT NO. 2005-04-I-TX REFINERY EXPLOSION AND FIRE TEXAS CITY, TEXAS MARCH 23, 2005 Page 73.
59 U.S. CHEMICAL SAFETY AND HAZARD INVESTIGATION BOARD INVESTIGATION RE-PORT. REPORT NO. 2005-04-I-TX REFINERY EXPLOSION AND FIRE TEXAS CITY, TEXAS MARCH 23, 2005 Page 76.

issues as they do not trust managers to take their concerns seriously. This view is born out of experience of being dismissed or, worse, belittled when they speak up.

Lack of meaningful response to reports discourages reporting. Texas City had a poor PSM incident investigation action item completion rate: only 33 percent were resolved at the end of 2004. The Telos report cited many stories of dangerous conditions persisting despite being pointed out to leadership, because "the unit cannot come down now." A 2001 safety assessment found "no accountability for timely completion and communication of reports."[60]

The lack of focus on key safety activities in Texas City was unacceptable in my opinion. However, the attitude displayed by the Executives in the case of the Herald of Free Enterprise when faced with safety concerns was terrifying. The memorandum referred to below was a request for indicator lights to be installed on the bridge of the ship to show when the bow doors were shut.

Mr. Develin circulated that memorandum amongst managers for comment. It was a serious memorandum which merited serious thought and attention, and called for a considered reply. The answers which Mr. Develin received will be set out verbatim. From Mr. J. F. Alcindor, a deputy chief superintendent: "Do they need an indicator to tell them whether the deck storekeeper is awake and sober? My goodness!!" From Mr. A. C. Reynolds: "Nice but don't we already pay someone!" From Mr. R. Ellison: "Assume the guy who shuts the doors tells the bridge if there is a problem." From Mr. D.

60 U.S. CHEMICAL SAFETY AND HAZARD INVESTIGATION BOARD INVESTIGATION REPORT. REPORT NO. 2005-04-I-TX REFINERY EXPLOSION AND FIRE TEXAS CITY, TEXAS MARCH 23, 2005 Page 181.

R. Hamilton: "Nice!" It is hardly necessary for the Court to comment that these replies display an absence of any proper sense of responsibility. Moreover the comment of Mr. Alcindsor on the deck storekeeper was either ominously prescient or showed an awareness of this type of incident in the past. If the sensible suggestion that indicator lights be installed had received, in 1985, the serious consideration which it deserved, it is at least possible that they would have been fitted in the early months of 1986 and this disaster might well have been prevented.[61]

Enough has been said to make it clear that by the autumn of 1986 the shore staff of the Company were well aware of the possibility that one of their ships would sail with her stern or bow doors open. They were also aware of a very sensible and simple device in the form of indicator lights which had been suggested by responsible Masters. That it was a sensible suggestion is now self-evident from the fact that the Company has installed indicator lights in their ships. That it was simple is illustrated by the fact that within a matter of days after the disaster indicator lights were installed in the remaining Spirit class ships and other ships of the fleet.[62]

Having dismissed safety-related reports and concerns, the management team took the issue seriously only after the fatal accident. This theme is evident in all of the incidents covered in this book.

---

61 HERALD OF FREE ENTERPRISE Report of Court No. 8074 Page 24 and 25.
62 HERALD OF FREE ENTERPRISE Report of Court No. 8074 Page 24 and 25.

Failure to Complete Safety Actions

Safety audits or reports which could have provided the opportunity to catch potential causes of future events and take action are ignored or not actioned in a timely fashion. I have witnessed, with alarming regularity, the findings of such audits go unaddressed. This has been for a number of reasons:

- Lack of respect for the auditors and, therefore, their findings
- Lack of time/willingness/ability to really get to grips with and understand the findings
- Denial of the issues identified
- Believing that because "we are the experts in our field, no one can tell us how to do our job"
- A belief that "it has always been done like that and it has always been okay"
- Failure to allocate sufficient resources to tackle the issues found.

It is now necessary to go back in time briefly. In 1982 the passenger ferry **EUROPEAN GATEWAY**, which was also owned by the Company, capsized after a collision off Harwich. Following that casualty the Company instituted an investigation into passenger safety. As a result of that investigation, on the 10th of February 1983, Captain Martin sent a report to Mr. Develin. That report was seen by Mr. Ayers. It begins with the words:

> The Company and ships' Masters could be considered negligent on the following points, particularly when some are the direct result of "commercial interests".
>
> (a) The ship's draught is not read before sailing, and the draught entered into the Official Log Book

is completely erroneous. (Against this was written "Policy".)

(b) It is not standard practice to inform the Master of his passenger figure before sailing.

(The written comment was "system informs Master, who often does not agree the truth of the information. Working practice".)

(c) The tonnage of cargo is not declared to the Master before sailing. (The comment against this was "working practice".)

(d) Full speed is maintained in dense fog. (Against this the comment was "policy".)[63]

Except for the recommendation relating to fog, all of these conditions still existed when the Herald of Free Enterprise accident occurred. It appears that Airgas also failed to implement a series of safety actions which, as was the case in the Herald of Free Enterprise, were aimed at preventing the very accident that they experienced.

Notably missing from the Airgas files on previous incidents, however, are the nitrous oxide safety guidelines that Scaled Composites publicly issued in July 2009.

Furthermore, no records provided by Airgas to the CSB[64] indicate the company ever considered or developed a program to follow important recommendations in the Scaled Composites safety guidelines, such as:

- Test for ignition sources, including friction, static discharge, or impact;

63 HERALD OF FREE ENTERPRISE Report of Court No. 8074 Page 27.
64 [U.S. Chemical Safety and Hazard Investigation Board]

- Ensure no component could exceed a temperature of 571°F;
- Evaluate compatibility of elastomers, plastics, metals, and lubricants;
- Remove all incompatible materials from a nitrous oxide flow path;
- Eliminate all corrosion prone metals from nitrous oxide flow path or storage; and
- Design pressure vessels, such as storage tanks or trailers, to provide a controlled vent during an overpressure event, to prevent a catastrophic vessel failure.

In 2003, CCPS[65] published Essential Practices for Managing Chemical Reactivity Hazards, an industry consensus guidance document specifically aimed at protecting workers and the public from uncontrolled chemical reactions, such as the decomposition of nitrous oxide. CCPS states that managing chemical reactivity hazards is not a "one-time" activity. Rather, effective management of reactivity hazards requires a continual management commitment to protect against the potential consequence of chemical reactivity incidents. Such a commitment includes an on-going effort to learn and incorporate key lessons from other major accidents. In addition, CCPS provided specific guidance to address reactivity hazards within a company's safety management system.[66]

In the case of Nimrod XV230, even after the fatal accident, actions were not completed to a satisfactory standard for a

---

65 [Centre for Chemical Process Safety]
66 Nitrous Oxide Explosion - Airgas (Air Liquide) Cantonment, Florida August 28, 2016 - U.S. Chemical Safety and Hazard Investigation Board Investigation Report One Killed Report Number: 2016-04-I-FL Issue Date: February 2017 Page 96.

number of years, during which the Nimrod fleet continued to operate.

It is a matter of concern that, despite the focus on fuel coupling leaks since the loss of XV230 almost three years ago, and the specific recommendations made by the BOI[67], documentation specifying fuel system maintenance should still have been regarded as inadequate in 2008.[68]

While the actions remain incomplete, the issue and therefore risk still exists, so other mitigating actions are required to enable safe operation until the root cause of the incident is addressed. Although the timeliness of corrective action completion is important, it should not be at the expense of the quality of the action taken to address the issue.

One of DuPont's process safety metrics was tracking the completion of corrective action items. However, this metric addressed only one aspect of the site's corrective action program—time needed to close the corrective action. Time to close corrective actions can indicate the priority management gives to completion of corrective action items. DuPont La Porte's focus on time to complete, however, sometimes resulted in closing action items after developing a plan to correct a deficiency rather than actually correcting it. *Guidelines for Risk-Based Process Safety* CCPS[69] states, "A safety management system can be seriously deficient, yet appear satisfactory by superficial measures—the paperwork appears to be in place and no serious incidents have been recorded. Complacency replaces

---

67 [Board of Inquiry]
68 The Nimrod Review Page 82.
69 [Centre for Chemical Process Safety]

a sense of vulnerability, and the execution of program tasks becomes perfunctory."[70]

Busy people, if given this way out, can, without malice, close out actions with promissory statements or "a plan for a plan". When this is done, nothing is fixed, and without the countdown clock to show that the action is incomplete and overdue, attention shifts to the next thing, and this issue is forgotten until a repeat event occurs.

Personal bonus objectives which state "zero overdue actions" can also drive a focus on the timeliness of closeout as opposed to the effectiveness of the action in removing the hazard. Both the issue of a "plan for a plan" and ineffective action closeout become more likely if people do not believe in the need for the action in the first place. As seen in King's Cross and NASA.

> Mr Lawrence testified that as his predecessors and senior managers had been satisfied with the processes in place, he would have found it very difficult to say that the system in place was inadequate. Yet a series of reports from within London Underground and from outside had repeatedly drawn attention both to the lack of training in emergency procedures and to the fire hazards on the system.[71]

> In the aftermath of the Challenger accident, these contradictory forces prompted a resistance to externally imposed changes and an attempt to maintain the internal belief that NASA was still a "perfect place," alone in its ability to execute a program of human space flight. Within NASA centers, as Human Space Flight Program managers strove to maintain their view of the

---

70 Toxic Chemical Release at the DuPont La Porte Chemical Facility Page 96.
71 Investigation into the King's Cross Underground Fire King's Cross Page 29.

organization, they lost their ability to accept criticism, leading them to reject the recommendations of many boards and blue-ribbon panels, the Rogers Commission among them. [72]

The leaders in King's Cross and NASA believed that because they were the specialists in their respective fields, they knew better than anyone else how to operate. Indeed, this arrogance or belief that ours is "a perfect place" and "we are the experts and so what would someone from outside know?" is more common than most would like to admit.

---

72 Columbia Accident Investigation Board Page 102.

Chapter 4
Hear No Evil, See No Evil, Speak No Evil

As senior business leaders, we can fall foul of confirmation bias and misinterpreting situations or data. We hear, see and say what we want to be the truth, not necessarily what is reality. We subconsciously misinterpret our Key Performance Indicators (KPIs), silence opposing views, mistake being busy for being effective and focus only on what is going well. In this chapter, I have taken what I believe to be the most common examples of this found in the events in question. They are:

- Success-based optimism
- Ineffective oversight
- Measuring the wrong things/misinterpreting data
- Target fixation
- Personal safety focus

Success-Based Optimism

In the previous chapter, we covered the consequences of failing to resolve known problems. In this chapter, we will look at some of the reasons that known issues are not addressed.

When known problems are not resolved, procedures are not followed or systems or processes fail, if there are no negative consequences and the aim is achieved, people become conditioned by success. This "turns the experience of failure into the memory of success": you have experienced a failure in your arrangements, and yet you were successful. Over time, having not corrected the parts that failed (because you were successful), you are exposed to risk which may one day result in a significant event.

This conditioning was, in my opinion, the route of the loss of Nimrod XV230. The Safety Case project to assess risks associated with the aircraft and make recommendations to address them was, from the outset, framed as a checkbox exercise. The prevailing view was that, given the age of the aircraft and its safety record, it must be safe. Unfortunately, given the small number of aircraft when compared with a passenger aircraft, there was not sufficient data to make this assumption.

> The suggestion that hazards with "seemingly unacceptable" Hazard Risk Indices could nevertheless "be considered for acceptance based on 20 years' historical evidence, as per Harrier[73] Safety Case", gives cause for concern. It indicates a flawed mindset for legacy aircraft: "If it has not happened in the past, it is unlikely to happen in the future." Further, as will be seen, the Nimrod fleet did not have sufficient total flight hours to provide a satisfactory historical incident base.[74]

This assumption led to complacency, which meant that the safety assessments were not completed with the required rigour and the deadline for completion of the project became more important than the quality of the work. When time got tight, corners were cut. The very hazard which caused the loss of the aircraft was highlighted as "catastrophic", but

---

73 [Another type of aircraft]
74 The Nimrod Review Page 194.

no mitigating actions were recommended or conducted.

A similar situation existed with the mindset of those charged with the safety of Columbia. "Foam shedding" from the large fuel tank mounted below the shuttle was a violation of design principles, as it was thought that the foam could damage the heat shield. Despite this, managers repeatedly authorized shuttle launches knowing that foam strikes had occurred frequently since the beginning of the shuttle program, often damaging the heat shield. Work was conducted over many years to prevent the foam detaching from the fuel tank, but while this work was ongoing, the shuttle continued to fly. On most occasions, the damage to the heat shield was considered to be minor, and so it became a maintenance issue as opposed to a safety-of-flight issue as per design.

> Anomalies that did not lead to catastrophic failure were treated as a source of valid engineering data that justified further flights. These anomalies were translated into a safety margin that was extremely influential, allowing engineers and managers to add incrementally to the amount and seriousness of damage that was acceptable.[75]

Even after it was clear from the launch videos that foam had struck the Orbiter in a manner never before seen, Space Shuttle Program managers were not unduly alarmed. They could not imagine why anyone would want a photo of something that could be fixed after landing. More importantly, learned attitudes to foam strikes diminished management's wariness of their danger. The Shuttle Program turned "the experience of failure into the memory of success." Managers also

---

75 Columbia Accident Investigation Board Page 196.

failed to develop simple contingency plans for a re-entry emergency. They were convinced, without study, that nothing could be done about such an emergency. The intellectual curiosity and skepticism that a solid safety culture requires was almost entirely absent. Shuttle managers did not embrace safety-conscious attitudes. Instead, their attitudes were shaped and reinforced by an organization that, in this instance, was incapable of stepping back and gauging its biases. Bureaucracy and process trumped thoroughness and reason.[76]

As mentioned in the previous chapter, the NASA team had the good fortune to have an early warning of how dangerous foam shedding could be. Unfortunately, they did not heed the warning. On a flight before the loss of Columbia, a piece of foam struck the heat shield of the shuttle. The shield was breached and so did not provide the thermal protection required to ensure a safe re-entry into the earth's atmosphere. On this occasion, the shuttle returned safely, not by good design or good management, but by good luck. The damage to the shield just happened to occur in an area where a small thick metal plate was behind the shield. This plate was not intended to provide thermal protection, but fortunately, it was able to do so. The plate stopped hot gases entering the structure of the shuttle and so prevented the loss of the spacecraft. Had the damage occurred almost anywhere else on the heat shield, the shuttle and its crew would almost certainly have been lost. Despite this "near miss", foam strikes continued to be viewed as a minor maintenance issue until the loss of Columbia.

As I mentioned previously, in the case of the King's Cross fire, it was believed that fires were an unavoidable fact of

76 Columbia Accident Investigation Board Page 181.

life when running an underground service, just as foam shedding was inevitable in shuttle operations. London Underground had a long history of fires, so the dangers posed by fire were trivialized; they were not referred to as fires but as "smoulderings". No one had been killed or seriously injured, so they may have taken the view that they had been successful in managing the hazards posed by fire.

I referred in chapter 4 "The Ethos of London Underground" to the received wisdom that fires on the Underground were inevitable. I can summarize the views of the directors of London Underground thus:

> No one in London Underground, either in recent years or for generations past, had foreseen that a fire starting on a wooden escalator could develop at a speed or with a ferocity which would endanger passengers.

> Whilst there had been some escalator fires in the past which had caused severe smoke, no passengers had ever been burned, and the true danger of smoke to people had never been foreseen.

> It was solely considerations of damage to escalators and disruption to services and not of danger to passenger safety which had dictated the action or lack of action by London Underground management.[77]

Given this attitude toward fire and its associated hazards, it is no surprise that a disaster such as took place on the night of the18th of November 1987 occurred. It is perhaps a surprise that it did not happen sooner.

---

77 Investigation into the King's Cross Underground Fire King's Cross Page 118.

Ineffective Oversight

An independent oversight function or equivalent should ensure that those in delivery or the front line don't do dangerous things or make improper decisions. They are the conscience of the organisation. Often, however, they are weak, disrespected and lacking in credibility. They are often staffed with people who lack experience that would lend them credibility, have little authority and are viewed as an unnecessary blocker as opposed to a respected oversight entity. In the case of NASA, the oversight functions were found to be ineffective after the loss of the space shuttle Challenger in 1986 and again following the loss of Columbia.

> The last line of defence against errors is usually a safety system. But the previous policy decisions by leaders described in chapter 5 also impacted the safety structure and contributed to both accidents. Neither in the O-ring erosion nor the foam debris problems did NASA's safety system attempt to reverse the course of events. In 1986, the Rogers Commission called it "The Silent Safety System." Pre-Challenger budget shortages resulted in safety personnel cutbacks. Without clout or independence, the safety personnel who remained were ineffective. In the case of Columbia, the Board found the same problems were reproduced and for an identical reason: when pressed for cost reduction, NASA attacked its own safety system.[78]

Having learned the lessons of the loss of Challenger, they quickly forgot them when cost pressures began to mount. This is a seemingly easy option. When faced with pressure to cut costs, the "soft services" come under fire.

---

78 Columbia Accident Investigation Board Page 199.

In my experience, there is often little thought for the consequences, particularly when a functional area is not respected.

Even when an oversight function is appropriately staffed, the lack of respect for the function they perform can render them ineffective. The relationship between QinetiQ, who were expected to provide an oversight function, and the Nimrod Integrated Project Team (IPT) is a good example of this. QinetiQ had been tasked with being the "independent confidence of the IPT", but it appears they were not capable of fulfilling the independent oversight role. This may have been due to their desire to gain further contracts, or incompetence. Either way, they were treated with disdain, and their presence was viewed as a tick in the box.

> George Baber, who complained that QinetiQ had not been consistent in its review of various safety case reports (relating to specific modifications and installations) said he had warned QinetiQ about this several times. Martyn Mahy recalls George Baber saying, "I don't need to get independent safety advice from QinetiQ, I can go elsewhere," referring to "bloody QinetiQ" and saying, "QinetiQ is just touting for business." (George Baber and other members of the IPT[79] denied that any hostility was displayed towards QinetiQ, but QinetiQ's version of events is well-supported by the contemporaneous documents). Frank Walsh said that he had had to put Witness L [QinetiQ] "back in his box" recently. Another member of the Nimrod IPT referred to the content of some of QinetiQ's reports as "Tosh!" George Baber told Martyn Mahy that QinetiQ would be able to comment on the NSC[80] when it was completed in March 2003.

79 [IPT – Integrated Project Team]
80 [Nimrod Safety Case]

After the meeting, Martyn Mahy spoke to Frank Walsh who said he was surprised at the "viciousness" of the IPTL's[81] comments about QinetiQ. Frank Walsh said in his evidence to the Review that the relationship with QinetiQ was the subject of some "tension" at this time because it was felt by the Nimrod IPT "that QinetiQ's recommendations were often influenced by a desire to generate more work and income for themselves".[82]

Faced with this level of hostility and perhaps sensing a need to maintain a relationship with their client, QinetiQ became ineffective.

QinetiQ's approach was fundamentally lax and compliant. QinetiQ failed at any stage to act as the independent "conscience" of the IPT[83]. As a result, the "third stool" in the safety process, namely independent assurance, was effectively missing from the Nimrod Safety Case process.[84]

As with Columbia, they were not viewed with respect, they were not provided with the information they needed to fulfil their obligations and they were not invited to critical meetings. This is not uncommon in my experience. The delivery line views the safety functions as people who are simply generating work for the delivery line to do, without any thought for the workload this places. As a result, the delivery line can become resentful and roll out acrimonious statements along the lines of, "You offer advice," and, "I don't have to take your advice."

This fractured relationship is commonly found in businesses that suffer from a desk-based oversight function. The lack of

---

81 [IPTL – Integrated Project Team Leader]
82 The Nimrod Review Page 212.
83 [Integrated Project Team]
84 The Nimrod Review Page 262.

presence "in the field" can lead to inaccurate audit findings which lack context. This further damages the credibility of the oversight function, increases resentment and ultimately can result in an ineffective oversight function. Audits conducted remotely are more likely to miss key findings and can become overly reliant on the honesty of those being audited. This was evident in the Piper Alpha incident, particularly in the areas of emergency training and the Permit to Work (PTW) system. The PTW system should keep people and equipment safe while maintenance activities are being carried out. Typically, it will involve risk assessments, methods to isolate energy (electricity, steam, chemicals, etc.) and instructions on how the work should be conducted.

> The evidence which I considered in chapter 11 showed that this failure was not an isolated mistake but that in a number of respects the PTW [85]system was being operated routinely in a casual and unsafe manner. That evidence along with the evidence to which I have referred earlier in this chapter shows, in my view, the operation of the PTW system was not being adequately monitored or audited. These were failures for which management were responsible. If there had been adequate monitoring and auditing it is likely that these deficiencies in the PTW system would have been corrected.[86]

Even when auditors are deployed "in the field" to look for deficiencies they can fail to find key and, at times, obvious shortfalls. This can be due to several factors, including a lack of the necessary experience required to see problems and the criteria used during the audits being overly

---

85 [Permit to Work]
86 The Public Inquiry Into the Piper Alpha Disaster Volume 1 Page 231.

restrictive. This leads to a blinkered audit or a focus on the wrong things. This is likely to have been the case in DuPont La Porte, where Process Safety Management (PSM) issues that had existed for some time were not identified.

> DuPont La Porte's first-party PSM[87] compliance audits, which were divided over a three-year cycle, took 68 auditor-days to complete between 2012 and 2014. These audits, however, did not identify or effectively correct long-standing PSM deficiencies in DuPont La Porte's process safety management system (e.g., deficiencies in performing process hazard analysis and management of change).[88]

Another potential reason for a lack of meaningful audit findings is that the business unit has learned how to "play the game". They know what the questions are and are able to convince the auditor that all is well. One method of achieving this is to swamp the auditor with information to "keep them busy", knowing that they have limited time. This is not uncommon, particularly when the results of audits are published company-wide or briefs are delivered to the superiors of the business unit head. There is a clear motivation to "get a good result", as few people want to look bad in front of the boss. Unfortunately, this desire to look good results in a lost opportunity: the opportunity to find out what your gaps to excellence are and resolve them.

Measuring the Wrong Things/Misinterpreting Data

The old adage "You get what you measure" has been proven time and again. This can be a good thing; it allows us to focus the organisation on key goals. It can, however, lead to negative results, particularly when we are misled

---

87 [Process Safety Management]
88 Toxic Chemical Release at the DuPont La Porte Chemical Facility Page 61.

by incomplete data sets or measuring the wrong things. There are often unintended consequences driven by our KPI sets and how our people are incentivised. Heavily weighted incentivisation programs can lead to a focus on the thing that would provide the largest financial return. In the case of Texas City, cost reduction had been weighted at 50 percent and safety performance, or Getting Health, Safety and the Environment Right (GHSER) programme performance, at 10 percent. This sheds light on what was important to the senior leadership team.

BP incorporated the Refining and Marketing GHSER[89] performance targets in performance contracts with business units and personal contracts with Group and business unit leadership. The performance contracts were used to evaluate personnel and impacted managers' compensation. The contracts consisted of weighted metrics for categories such as financial performance, plant reliability, and safety. The largest percentage of the weighting was in financial outcome and cost reduction. The safety metrics included fatalities, days away from work case rate, recordable injuries, and vehicle accidents; process safety metrics were not included. HSE[90] metrics typically accounted for less than 20 percent of the total weighting in the performance contracts. BP Group implemented an incentive program based on performance metrics, the Variable Pay Plan (VPP), which was in place at the Texas City refinery for several years prior to the ISOM incident. Payouts under the VPP were approved by the refining executive managers in London. "Cost leadership" categories accounted for 50 percent and

---

89 [Getting Health Safety and Environment Right]
90 [Health and Safety Executive]

safety metrics for 10 percent of the total bonus. For the 2003-2004 period, the single safety metric for the VPP bonus was the OSHA[91] Recordable Injury Rate.[92]

Incentives are intended to drive worker behaviour. They tell people what is important to the leadership of the business and reward them for focusing on those important things.

BP Group managers failed to provide effective leadership and oversight to control major accident risk. According to Hopkins, top management's actions and what they paid attention to, measure and allocate resources for is what drives organizational culture (Hopkins, 2005). Examples of deficient leadership at Texas City included managers not following or ensuring enforcement of policies and procedures, responding ineffectively to a series of reports detailing critical process safety problems, and focusing on budget cutting goals that compromised safety.[93]

It can be said that we want our people to carry out all aspects of their work to a satisfactory standard and that incentives are merely a way of encouraging people to pay particular attention to certain aspects while still doing all aspects to a satisfactory standard. Unfortunately, this is not always the case. Whether consciously or otherwise, people will focus on what is perceived to be the most important thing. It doesn't have to include a financial reward. If we measure and pay attention to a specific aspect above all

91 [Occupational Safety and Health Act]
92 U.S. CHEMICAL SAFETY AND HAZARD INVESTIGATION BOARD INVESTIGATION REPORT. REPORT NO. 2005-04-I-TX REFINERY EXPLOSION AND FIRE TEXAS CITY, TEXAS MARCH 23, 2005 Page 153).
93 U.S. CHEMICAL SAFETY AND HAZARD INVESTIGATION BOARD INVESTIGATION REPORT. REPORT NO. 2005-04-I-TX REFINERY EXPLOSION AND FIRE TEXAS CITY, TEXAS MARCH 23, 2005 Page 187.

others, the people we lead are likely to focus on that thing. They will receive positive strokes if it is performing well and unwanted focus if it is not.

[I]n performance year 2011, the DuPont La Porte site established the safety modifier based on the number of OSHA total recordable injuries, with the number of recordable injuries causing a reduction in available incentive award payments that were otherwise due to be paid to members of that portion of the workforce. Specifically, at the program's start in 2011, if there were three or fewer recordable injuries, the LPBC[94] set the safety modifier value at 1, which did not reduce the incentive payable for business performance; however, as more recordable injuries occurred, the safety modifier incrementally reduced the total incentive paid to employees. By using a safety modifier that considered only worker injuries, DuPont La Porte equated safety performance with occupational safety metrics, similar to DuPont's Safety Perception Surveys. Thus, DuPont La Porte did not include a process safety performance metric in its incentive. A disproportionate emphasis on occupational safety metrics as the measurement for safety performance could confuse personnel into viewing occupational safety and process safety as the same or perceiving that occupational safety is more important than process safety. Furthermore, emphasizing a low number of total recordable injuries could give personnel false confidence about process safety performance. "Money is one of the strongest influences on human behavior, for better or worse. When developing compensation and incentive schemes based on process safety performance, it is critical to

---

94 [Local Performance Based Compensation program]

design them carefully to reinforce the desired cultural attributes and behaviors. It is equally critical to be aware of the many pitfalls that lead a well-intentioned compensation scheme to unwittingly support negative behaviors."[95]

There is a fine balance to be had in the way we react to successes and failures. An overly negative response to issues with the intent of improving performance can drive the reporting of issues underground. People become reluctant to report small issues for fear of being sanctioned. This can result in the loss of opportunities to correct minor deviations before they become more serious.

> DuPont La Porte's Employee Incentive Program. The DuPont La Porte bonus structure may have disincentivized workers from reporting injuries, incidents, and "near misses." Ensuring that employees can report injuries or incidents in accordance with the Occupational Safety and Health (OSH) Act and OSHA regulations, without fear of discrimination, retaliation, or other adverse consequence is central to protecting worker safety and health, and aiding accident prevention.[96]

While leading a leadership peer review, I had a conversation about safety and the reporting of near-miss events with a contractor. I was surprised when he freely admitted that he and his team did not report safety issues or events. He went on to explain that his contract was written in such a way that if he and his company had safety events, they would have payments deducted. On the face of it, the intent of the contract was right: in being penalized for poor safety performance, the contractor would ensure that

---

95 Toxic Chemical Release at the DuPont La Porte Chemical Facility Page 116.
96 Toxic Chemical Release at the DuPont La Porte Chemical Facility Page 11.

improvements were made. Unfortunately, that was not the outcome. In failing to report minor safety concerns, the opportunity to resolve issues when they resulted in no safety consequence is removed. The next opportunity is when they do have a safety consequence.

The lack of reporting could give a false indication that all is well. The same can be said for measuring the wrong things in DuPont La Porte. Their Safety Perception Survey was certainly limited and potentially misleading.

DuPont La Porte used a proprietary Safety Perception Survey that focused on personal or occupational safety but did not evaluate or assess the process safety culture. Because the Safety Perception Survey did not reasonably evaluate all safety aspects of culture, it could not help identify the significant process safety weaknesses at the DuPont La Porte facility, leaving the site vulnerable to potential process safety incidents. While measuring worker perceptions of personal safety is important, a safety culture assessment program should also provide an effective gauge of process safety.[97]

The results of this survey could well give a false indication of good performance overall, particularly when the management team probably wanted to see a positive answer to the question asked. Unfortunately, there is often a difference between the Key Performance Question (KPQ) that has been asked and the way the KPI (the answer to the KPQ) is interpreted. In the case of Columbia, they were caught out.

At the Flight Readiness Review for the next mission, Orbiter Project management reported that, based on the completion of repairs to the Orbiter Thermal

---

97 Toxic Chemical Release at the DuPont La Porte Chemical Facility Page 11.

Protection System, the bipod ramp foam loss In-Flight Anomaly was resolved, or "closed." However, although the closure documents detailed the repairs made to the Orbiter, neither the Certificate of Flight Readiness documentation nor the Flight Readiness Review documentation referenced correcting the cause of the damage — the shedding of foam.[98]

A good indication that there may be problems with your metrics is when everything in your KPI set is green and yet you are having safety issues. Perhaps you are told that the foam loss has been resolved and yet you continue to lose foam. One option is to dismiss the safety issues as one-offs, as the KPIs are green. The other is to question if you are measuring the wrong things.

During another leadership peer review, my team found that *manager in the field* statistics (an in-the-field audit of worker behaviour) showed very good schedule adherence. The scores for the use of core human performance tools were also consistently high. This gave the impression of good worker safety performance. This data was used to argue that no action was required, despite several near-miss incidents. When we looked more closely, the Excel spreadsheet had not been updated for some time, as the person responsible for doing so had moved on. The graphs simply used the last data entered and projected the same scores forward, giving the impression of solid and stable performance.

Target Fixation

The phrase *target fixation* was commonly used in the Second World War to describe a deadly phenomenon. Fighter bomber pilots would become so focused on the

98 Columbia Accident Investigation Board Page 123.

ground target they were attacking that they would fly into the ground or would fail to realise that an enemy aircraft was behind them firing. The same effect exists in many situations in life, including business scenarios and contexts. A target or objective becomes so important that we devote all our efforts and attention to it, often without realising we are doing it. Other aspects of our business begin to suffer, and we do not notice until an adverse event snaps a failing aspect of our business back into our consciousness. By then it may be too late to avoid disaster.

In the case of the loss of Nimrod XV230, the Texas City accident and the loss of Columbia, the target in question was cost reduction. In each case, over several years, cost reduction initiatives had been stacked one upon another. I will cover this in more detail in a later chapter. (In the case of Nimrod XV230, *airworthiness* means the safety of the aircraft.)

"There was no doubt that the culture at the time had switched. In the days of Sir Colin Terry you had to be on top of airworthiness. By 2004, you had to be on top of your budget, if you wanted to get ahead" (former senior RAF officer, 2008). "Your friend the British soldier can stand up to anything except the British War Office" (George Bernard Shaw, 1856–1950, *The Devil's Disciple*, 1901). "We trained hard, but it seemed that every time we were beginning to form up into teams, we would be reorganized. I was to learn later in life that we tend to meet any new situation by reorganizing; and a wonderful method it can be for creating the illusion of progress while producing confusion, inefficiency, and demoralization" (Gaius Petronius Arbiter, 210 BC). Financial pressures (in the shape of "cuts", "savings", "efficiencies", "strategic targets", "reduction in output costs", "leaning", etc.) drove a cascade of multifarious organisational changes (called variously "change", "initiatives", "change initiatives", "transformation", "re-energizing", etc.) which led to a dilution of the airworthiness regime and culture within the MOD and distraction from safety and airworthiness issues. There was a shift in culture and priorities in the MOD[99] towards "business" and financial targets, at the expense of functional values such as safety and airworthiness. The Defence Logistics Organization, in particular, came under huge pressure. Its primary focus became delivering "change" and the "change programme" and achieving the "Strategic Goal" of a 20 percent reduction in output costs in five years and other financial savings.[100]

In addition to year-on-year budget cuts, the Columbia team faced a different but no less all-consuming target: schedule adherence. The shuttle programme was key to the construction of the International Space Station (ISS). Given the importance and global profile of the ISS, NASA had to deliver.

This chapter connects Chapter 5's analysis of NASA's broader policy environment to a focused scrutiny of Space Shuttle Program decisions that led to the STS-107[101] accident. Section 6.1 illustrates how foam debris losses that violated design requirements came to be defined by NASA management as an acceptable aspect of Shuttle missions, one that posed merely a maintenance "turnaround" problem rather than a safety-of-flight concern. Section 6.2 shows how, at

---

99 [Ministry of Defence]
100 The Nimrod Review Page 355.
101 [Space Transport System – Flight/mission number]

a pivotal juncture just months before the Columbia accident, the management goal of completing Node 2 of the International Space Station on time encouraged Shuttle managers to continue flying, even after a significant bipod-foam debris strike on STS-112.[102]

Even in the face of undeniable violations in their own safety procedures, the management team chose to continue flight operations.

Schedules are essential tools that help large organizations effectively manage their resources. Aggressive schedules by themselves are often a sign of a healthy institution. However, other institutional goals, such as safety, sometimes compete with schedules, so the effects of schedule pressure in an organization must be carefully monitored. The Board posed the question: Was there undue pressure to nail the Node 2 launch date to the February 19, 2004, signpost? The management and workforce of the Shuttle and Space Station programs each answered the question differently. Various members of NASA upper management gave a definite "no." In contrast, the workforce within both programs thought there was considerable management focus on Node 2 and resulting pressure to hold firm to that launch date, and individuals were becoming concerned that safety might be compromised. The weight of evidence supports the workforce view.[103]

Members of the mission management team even described their own rationale for a previous launch as "lousy". These managers appear to have become fixated on launch schedules. The same managers were involved in the Columbia mission.

---

102 Columbia Accident Investigation Board Page 121.
103 Columbia Accident Investigation Board Page 131.

Interestingly, during Columbia's mission, the Chair of the Mission Management Team, Linda Ham, would characterize that reasoning as "lousy"—though neither she nor Shuttle Program Manager Ron Distemper, who were both present at the meeting, questioned it at the time. The pressing need to launch STS-113[104] to retrieve the International Space Station Expedition 5 crew before they surpassed the 180-day limit and to continue the countdown to Node 2 were surely in the back of managers' minds during these reviews. Even with work scheduled on holidays, a third shift of workers being hired and trained, future crew rotations drifting beyond 180 days, and some tests previously deemed "requirements" being skipped or deferred, Program managers estimated that Node 2 launch would be one to two months late. They were slowly accepting additional risk in trying to meet a schedule that probably could not be met. Interviews with workers provided insight into how this situation occurred. They noted that people who work at NASA have the legendary can-do attitude, which contributes to the agency's successes. But it can also cause problems. When workers are asked to find days of margin, they work furiously to do so and are praised for each extra day they find. But those same people (and this same culture) have difficulty admitting that something "can't" or "shouldn't" be done, that the margin has been cut too much, or that resources are being stretched too thin. No one at NASA wants to be the one to stand up and say, "We can't make that date." [105]

They knew that they didn't have a firm justification to fly.

104 [Space Transport System – Flight/mission number]
105 Columbia Accident Investigation Board Page 138.

They also knew that they had eroded the safety margins in several other areas, and yet they flew the mission. Such was the power of their target fixation. The same behavioural and cultural issues were evident in the Deepwater Horizon incident.

[A]t the time of the Macondo blowout, BP's corporate culture remained one that was embedded in risk-taking and cost-cutting—much like was found to be its case in 2005 (Texas City), in 2006 (Alaska North Slope Spill), and in 2010 ("The Spill"). Whether there is "evidence" that someone in the Macondo well project made a conscious decision to put costs before safety misses the more important point. It is the underlying safety culture, much of it so ingrained as to be unconscious, that governs the actions of an organization and its personnel. Cultural influences that permeate an organization and an industry and manifest in actions that can either promote and nurture a high-reliability organization with high-reliability systems, or actions reflective of complacency, excessive risk-taking, and a loss of team situational awareness. The multiple failures (to contain, control, mitigate, plan, and clean-up) that unfolded and ultimately drove this disaster appear to be deeply rooted in a multi-decade history of organizational malfunction and shortsightedness. There were multiple opportunities to properly assess the likelihoods and consequences of organizational decisions (i.e., Risk Assessment and Management) that were ostensibly driven by BP management's desire to "close the competitive gap" and improve bottom-line performance. Consequently, although there were multiple chances to do the right things in the right ways at the right times, management's perspective failed to recognize and accept its own fallibility despite a record of recent accidents in the U.S. and a series of promises to change BP's safety culture.[106]

It is all well and good saying that safety is your number one priority, but if you pay lip service to it and the workforce feels consistent pressure about schedule and/or costs, that is what is perceived to be important, so that is what your people focus on. "You can't talk your way out of a problem you behaved your way into!" (Stephen R. Covey)

Personal Safety Focus

When I refer to *personal safety*, I mean safety aspects that are concerned with worker safety and behavioural safety. This focuses very much on the person on the "front line"/"shop floor"/"coal face". It is concerned with "slips, trips and falls" and procedural compliance/violations at a shop floor level. This can be an attractive place to focus management attention because it is easy to measure and it is relatively cheap to improve, as can be seen in the example of Texas City.

A central component of the BP Texas City approach to safety was its behavioural programs, which had been in effect in some form since 1997. The program, based on observations of BP workers and contractors engaged in work tasks, was designed to provide immediate feedback about observed hazards and activities that did not conform to refinery safety policies.[107]

This is not bad practice so long as it forms *part of* your safety programme as opposed to *being* your safety programme.

106 Final Report on the Investigation of the Macondo Well Blowout Deepwater Horizon Study Group March 1, 2011 Page 87.

107 U.S. CHEMICAL SAFETY AND HAZARD INVESTIGATION BOARD INVESTIGATION RE-PORT. REPORT NO. 2005-04-I-TX REFINERY EXPLOSION AND FIRE TEXAS CITY, TEXAS MARCH 23, 2005 Page 153.

The management team in this instance was described as follows:

> At Texas City, workers perceived the managers as "too worried about seat belts" and too little about the danger of catastrophic accidents. Individual safety "was more closely managed because it 'counted' for or against managers on their current watch (along with budgets) and it was more acceptable to avoid costs related to integrity management because the consequences might occur later, on someone else's watch.[108]

Although very important, personal safety statistics can lull us into a false sense of security. It is easy to subconsciously view personal safety statistics as a representation of overall safety. They are often posted on notice boards, newsletters and websites as a way of showing just how safe a company is. Unfortunately, they only show one aspect of safety.

> In both cases—the BP Texas City and the BP Macondo well disasters—meetings were held with operations personnel at the same time and place the initial failures were developing. These meetings were intended to congratulate the operating crews and organizations for their excellent records for worker safety. Both of these disasters have served—as many others have served—to clearly show there are important differences between worker safety and system safety. One does not assure the other.[109]

> Personal safety metrics are important to track low-consequence, high-probability incidents, but are not

108 U.S. CHEMICAL SAFETY AND HAZARD INVESTIGATION BOARD INVESTIGATION RE-PORT. REPORT NO. 2005-04-I-TX REFINERY EXPLOSION AND FIRE TEXAS CITY, TEXAS MARCH 23, 2005 Page 175.
109 Final Report on the Investigation of the Macondo Well Blowout Deepwater Horizon Study Group March 1, 2011 Page 10.

a good indicator of process safety performance. As process safety expert Trevor Kletz notes, "The lost time rate is not a measure of process safety" (Kletz, 2003). An emphasis on personal safety statistics can lead companies to lose sight of deteriorating process safety performance (Hopkins, 2000).[110]

There is also the aspect of being misled by your metrics.

However, BP Group oversight and Texas City management focused on personal safety rather than on process safety and preventing catastrophic incidents. Financial and personal safety metrics largely drove BP Group and Texas City performance, to the point that BP managers increased performance site bonuses even in the face of the three fatalities in 2004. Except for the 1,000-day goals, site business contracts, manager performance contracts, and VPP[111] bonus metrics were unchanged as a result of the 2004 fatalities.[112]

This is a good example of falling for the seductive nature of personal safety metrics. The BP team was rewarded for improving safety because the metric for personal safety didn't include the fatalities. These, presumably, were in another KPI which didn't impact their annual bonus.

Just because no one in your workforce has tripped over a paving slab recently does not mean your maintenance arrangements are robust in preventing a loss of containment of a hazardous chemical. It does not mean that your processes have been effectively implemented

110 U.S. CHEMICAL SAFETY AND HAZARD INVESTIGATION BOARD INVESTIGATION RE-PORT. REPORT NO. 2005-04-I-TX REFINERY EXPLOSION AND FIRE TEXAS CITY, TEXAS MARCH 23, 2005 Page 185.
111 [Variable Pay Plan]
112 U.S. CHEMICAL SAFETY AND HAZARD INVESTIGATION BOARD INVESTIGATION RE-PORT. REPORT NO. 2005-04-I-TX REFINERY EXPLOSION AND FIRE TEXAS CITY, TEXAS MARCH 23, 2005 Page 178.

and are being complied with at all levels of your business.

For more than a decade, DuPont developed and honed a safety culture program to reduce its OSHA[113] total recordable injury rate by assessing and improving occupational (personal) safety, using its Bradley Curve and Safety Perception Survey tools (Appendix E). These tools, however, focus on only one aspect of safety culture—personal safety. DuPont La Porte used the Safety Perception Survey without doing a process safety culture assessment as recommended in the corporate process safety management standard. Because this survey did not formally assess process safety culture perceptions, DuPont La Porte never evaluated its process safety culture. Had its efforts included a focus on perceptions of process safety as well as personal safety in its Safety Perception Survey, or had it performed a separate process safety culture assessment with the intent of improving process safety culture as recognized in DuPont's corporate process safety management standard, DuPont La Porte likely would have been more aware of potential process safety issues and better positioned to prevent or mitigate future process safety incidents. CCPS[114] recognizes the importance of a strong process safety culture in preventing major accidents.[115]

A personal safety focus centred around worker behaviours can set the tone for how your business views safety shortfalls. Through the personal safety lens, any event could be considered to be a "human act". That may be human error, a deliberate violation or some other thing that can be pinned on the individual or team.

---

113 [Occupational Safety and Health Act]
114 [Centre for Chemical Process Safety]
115 Toxic Chemical Release at the DuPont La Porte Chemical Facility Page 80.

When we view safety from this perspective, we can become blind to the significant hazards that exist in process or "plant" safety and procedural safety. When this happens, we fail to recognise when management action, or lack thereof, has contributed to or caused an accident. We can happily dismiss the failure of a pipe or other piece of equipment as a one-off because most of our accidents, high-frequency, low-consequence, are the result of personal choice or worker behaviour.

The use of the phrase *personal choice* is the comfort zone of many a leader. In using this phrase as a leader I am saying that everything I was responsible for was done correctly. The individual knew what was expected, they were trained correctly, they had everything they needed to do the task correctly but chose not to do so.

This is the area that requires careful thought. There are, of course, genuine violations. They are committed for any number of reasons. However, as I briefly mentioned in the last chapter, there are also things that James Reason refers to as "necessary violations" and other causes for "the bad thing" to happen on the shop floor. Most of these things do not point at the shop floor worker; they point to management failures.

> The Telos consultants also noted that concern about equipment conditions was expressed not only by BP personnel, but "strongly expressed by senior members" of the contracting community who "pointed out many specific hazards in the work environment that would not be found at other area plants." The consultants concluded that the tolerance of "these kind of risks must contribute to the tolerance of risks you see in individual behavior".[116]

116 U.S. CHEMICAL SAFETY AND HAZARD INVESTIGATION BOARD INVESTIGATION RE-

In this example, it was concluded that in tolerating degraded plant conditions, managers contributed to a culture in which behavioural deviance became normal. Not only was this situation thought of as being normal, because of the degraded material condition of the facility, but also it became essential. It was not possible to complete the tasks required "by the book", so workers developed workarounds to get the job done. These are known as *necessary violations*. I have listened to executives in board rooms who profess to have a policy of, "If in doubt, stop and make the facility safe." This message often does not land at the factory floor. The same leaders who say these kinds of things also, consciously or otherwise, exert pressure to achieve results despite known deficiencies in the condition of plant and equipment.

PORT. REPORT NO. 2005-04-I-TX REFINERY EXPLOSION AND FIRE TEXAS CITY, TEXAS MARCH 23, 2005 Page 175.

Chapter 5
The Perfect Place

In this chapter, we focus on the behaviours of leaders and how seemingly small behavioural traits can have significant impacts. It is easy to assume that our business performance is satisfactory without having verified that things are the way they should be. We can also fail to benchmark against other organisations to gain a different perspective. This is a common theme both in these events and in my experience.

Self-Referencing

There are many reasons why a business can become self-referencing. It can be that the business exists in a specialist field, the business founded the industry or cost-cutting leads to cuts in benchmarking and recruitment from outside of the organisation. In some industries, people move up through the ranks as a matter of course within the same business. While they will have a great deal of experience, they will not necessarily have a breadth of view, as was the case in London Underground.

> In both the Operations and the Engineering Directorates there had been a tradition of very long service. Many of the witnesses from London Underground had spent their entire working lives with the company and been promoted through the ranks largely on the basis of seniority.

Very few staff failed the training course which qualified them for promotion after a given length of service. Conversely, there was no means for anyone who was talented and ambitious to be promoted before his qualifying period. Few junior staff held professional or public examination qualifications. Indeed the Operations Director accepted that it was likely that there was nobody who had a nationally recognised qualification at King's Cross station on 18 November 1987, when they were responsible for perhaps £40 million worth of assets and a quarter of a million passengers.

Only 5 percent of management-level posts were advertised externally, and appointments from outside the organisation were rare. In the specialised areas of the Engineering Directorate, Mr Lawrence argued that there were unlikely to be better resources available outside London Underground. He did accept that weaknesses in staff skill levels had been identified in 1987 in the Lift and Escalator Department and that improved training was still required. The opportunities for further education to allow staff to gain professional qualifications remained very limited.[117]

The collective lack of breadth of experience can lead to a misplaced confidence in our own arrangements. This, in turn, deepens the tendency to avoid or dismiss external feedback or advice. This is evidenced in the Piper Alpha incident report, specifically in relation to the Permit to Work process.

The quality of the laid-down permit procedure was the acknowledged responsibility of management, and Mr

117 Investigation into the King's Cross Underground Fire King's Cross Page 30.

McReynolds in particular. Although that procedure was revised as recently as 1985 there appears to have been no attempt to assess whether it stood comparison with the systems of other operators or satisfied the guidelines available to the industry as a whole. In view of the wealth of experience available within Occidental it is hard to understand how there were critical and obvious omissions in the PTW[118] system, such as a method of locking off isolation valves to prevent inadvertent de-isolation. The managers who had responsibility for the correct operation of the PTW system were all aware that the safety personnel on the platform were expected to monitor the daily operation of the system. All of them assumed that because they received no reports of failings the system was working properly. However none of them checked the quality of that monitoring nor did they carry out more than the most cursory examination of permits when they had occasion to visit Piper. The lack of any critical reference to the PTW system in the audits which had been carried out on Piper reinforced the assumption that all was well. However it is difficult to understand how it came about that this auditing did not identify the deficiencies which so quickly became apparent in the course of evidence at the Inquiry. Mr Richards was evidently correct when he said that his conclusion was "that a proper audit system should be set up".[119]

The compounding issues of negative confirmation, where no news is good news, and a failure to seek industry best practice led to false confidence in London Underground. When benchmarking, external recruitment and consultancy

---

118 [Permit to Work]
119 The Public Inquiry Into the Piper Alpha Disaster Volume 1 Page 231.

are eliminated, external influence and learning can, over time, be viewed not just as unnecessary but as something to actively avoid.

This long-established and deeply rooted approach to staffing and training also had its effect on the ethos of London Underground. Staff tended to have narrow horizons and would instinctively look inside the organisation for advice and the solution to problems. Compartmental organisation resulted in little exchange of information or ideas between Departments, and still less cross-fertilisation with other industries and outside organisations. While on the one hand this inward-looking approach may have allowed London Underground to become preeminent in certain technical fields such as signal engineering, it undoubtedly led to a dangerous, blinkered self-sufficiency which included a general unwillingness to take advice or accept criticism from outside bodies. The Court heard, for example, about advice from the London Fire Brigade regarding the importance and procedure for calling them which went unheeded (see chapter 11, "The Response of the Emergency Services: London Fire Brigade"); and criticism of the quality of data and staff resources relating to occupational health and safety by the Health and Safety Executive's Accident Prevention Advisory Unit, upon which no action was taken.[120]

When a business is highly specialised, the attitude can be, "We are the industry leaders. Who could possibly tell us how to do our thing better?" and so advice and criticism are ignored. This is discussed in detail in the Nimrod report.

As Richard Oldfield told the Review: "We were very close

---

120 Investigation into the King's Cross Underground Fire King's Cross Page 31.

to Frank Walsh on this programme. The primary point of contact was Frank Walsh." This closeness manifested itself in a joint reluctance to accept criticism from third parties. This is illustrated, e.g., by BAE Systems' and Frank Walsh's response to an "Air Environment IPTs[121] Hazard Log Review" dated 7 April 2005 produced by Echelon Consulting Limited. The Echelon report noted inter alia (section B.4) that the "Nimrod IPT's reliance on the BAES Fault Tree has relegated Cassandra to a position where it is little more than a high-level management reporting tool" and that "the detail contained in the hazards and accidents descriptions is insufficient to reason about the legitimacy of the relationship". Frank Walsh sent a copy of the report to BAE Systems on 20 April 2005, prompting an angry response from Chris Lowe. That response was echoed by Frank Walsh who, on 26 April 2005, wrote to Chris Lowe stating, "I believe that I have returned Echelon to their box and screwed the lid on."[122]

The same culture existed in NASA. They also actively avoided or ignored external influences.

As a result, NASA's human space flight culture never fully adapted to the Space Shuttle Program, with its goal of routine access to space rather than further exploration beyond low-Earth orbit. The Apollo-era organizational culture came to be in tension with the more bureaucratic space agency of the 1970s, whose focus turned from designing new spacecraft at any expense to repetitively flying a reusable vehicle on an ever-tightening budget. This trend toward bureaucracy and the associated increased reliance on contracting

---

121 [Integrated Project Team]
122 The Nimrod Review Page 311.

necessitated more effective communications and more extensive safety oversight processes than had been in place during the Apollo era, but the Rogers Commission found that such features were lacking.

In the aftermath of the Challenger accident, these contradictory forces prompted a resistance to externally imposed changes and an attempt to maintain the internal belief that NASA was still a "perfect place," alone in its ability to execute a program of human space flight. Within NASA centers, as Human Space Flight Program managers strove to maintain their view of the organization, they lost their ability to accept criticism, leading them to reject the recommendations of many boards and blue-ribbon panels, the Rogers Commission among them.[123]

As the 21st century began, NASA's deeply ingrained human space flight culture—one that has evolved over 30 years as the basis for a more conservative, less technically and organizationally capable organization than the Apollo-era NASA—remained strong enough to resist external pressures for adaptation and change. At the time of the launch of STS-107[124], NASA retained too many negative (and also many positive) aspects of its traditional culture: "flawed decision making, self-deception, introversion and a diminished curiosity about the world outside the perfect place." These characteristics were reflected in NASA's less than stellar performance before and during the STS-107 mission, which is described in the following chapters.[125]

---

123 Columbia Accident Investigation Board Page 102.
124 [Space Transport System – Flight/mission number]
125 Columbia Accident Investigation Board Page 118.

In less specialised fields, a similar "self-referencing" tendency can also exist. Sugar dust explosion hazards are well known and the problem of establishing preventative measures has been solved many times. Despite this, it appears that the pitfall of trying to come up with their own solution resulted in a failure to take meaningful action and led to Imperial Sugar being exposed to the hazards for years.

This dust problem has become so serious and dangerous in modern refineries...at present, we have so much to correct that is knowingly wrong, there is no need for outside help. We make a lot of dust in the plant and have had a very inefficient dust collecting system[;] consequently, it has been hopeless to try to keep the dry end of our plant clean. We have heavy accumulations of dust in several areas... we hope to improve the house keeping around the silos.[126]

This memo was sent in 1967. A year later an explosion occurred, and unfortunately, this was neither the first nor the last incident in the facility.

Over the years, [there have been] combustible dust incidents at sugar refineries worldwide. In 1998, an employee was severely burned by a sugar dust explosion in the powdered sugar mill room at the Imperial Sugar refinery in Sugar Land, Texas. Yet, more than eight years after that incident the corporate safety manager wrote in a memo to senior management: "Based on conversations with the quality team at each location, we did not have a formal policy for sanitation/ housekeeping at any of our sites." Still, the draft

126 INVESTIGATION REPORT. Report No. 2008-05-I-GA September 2009 SUGAR DUST EXPLOSION AND FIRE Page 47.

sanitation/housekeeping policy attached to the memo did not discuss sugar dust. Management did not take adequate action to correct the long-standing hazardous combustible dust conditions in their facilities.[127]

Having suffered explosions and numerous fires in the years leading up to the 2008 fatal accident, it appears that the management team failed to adequately address issues that persisted for decades.

Port Wentworth facility management personnel were aware of sugar dust explosion hazards and emphasized the importance of properly designed dust handling equipment and good housekeeping practices to minimize dust accumulation as long ago as 1958, but did not take action to minimize and control sugar dust hazards.

Over the years, the facility experienced granulated sugar and powdered sugar fires caused by overheated bearings or electrical devices in the packing building. However, none of these incidents resulted in a devastating sugar dust explosion or major fire before the February 2008 incident.

Company management and the managers and workers at both the Port Wentworth, Georgia, and Gramercy, Louisiana, refineries did not recognize the significant hazard posed by sugar dust, despite the continuing history of near-misses.[128]

Despite knowing that they had a big issue and also knowing that dust causes explosions, they appear not to have put the two together, ie. We have a big problem that could cause

127 INVESTIGATION REPORT. Report No. 2008-05-I-GA September 2009 SUGAR DUST EXPLOSION AND FIRE Pages 48 and 49.
128 INVESTIGATION REPORT. Report No. 2008-05-I-GA September 2009 SUGAR DUST EXPLOSION AND FIRE Page 63

an explosion; we need to stop and get all the help we need to resolve the issues. Instead, it appears that an avoidance of solutions that were "not invented here", a tendency to avoid the ideas or standards of others, may have crept in. This, combined with a lack of "significant" incidents, may have led to the decision to continue to operate

Assumptions Based on Poor / No Data

Senior managers tend to make decisions based on limited or no data or assumptions. This is a necessary skill to have and is, in some circumstances, vital. However, it can be dangerous when it is done subconsciously or when it is done out of arrogance or bravado.

Sometimes the data is not obtainable in a reasonable timescale or with a proportionate level of effort. A "balance of probability" decision is needed, which considers the consequences of making the wrong decision against how much data is needed before making the call.

In each of the events considered here, the data was available and easily obtainable, as was the case in King's Cross.

> Major Rose[129] explained that he did not expect his inspecting officers to look at matters specific to fire protection, such as the existence of wood in escalator shafts, and the accumulation of grease and detritus. He said however that they drew some comfort from the inspections of stations and tunnels customarily made each year by the London Fire Brigade. But the Inspectorate stopped receiving copies of the London Fire Brigade's inspection reports in 1984 after the Inspectorate's accident officer had taken the view that the reports were being satisfactorily made and he need no longer see copies. Major Rose conceded that this

---

129 [The Chief Inspector of Railways]

was an unfortunate decision. The Inspectorate is now receiving copies of the reports and has received back copies of those it missed. The fact remains that there was no proper liaison between the Railway Inspectorate and the London Fire Brigade regarding their respective interests in safety on the London Underground.[130]

This approach is similar to that regarding the Permit to Work process on Piper Alpha, as previously discussed, and to that taken by the masters of the Herald of Free Enterprise: no news is good news.

Captain Lewry joined the Herald on 13 March 1980 as one of five masters. The Company has issued a set of standing orders which included the following:

> 01.09 **Ready for Sea** Heads of Departments are to report to the Master immediately they are aware of any deficiency which is likely to cause their departments to be unready for sea in any respect at the due sailing time. In the absence of any such report the Master will assume, at the due sailing time, that the vessel is ready for sea in all respects.

That order was unsatisfactory in many respects. It followed immediately after 01.08 which was an order that defects had to be reported to the Head of Department. The sequence of orders raises at least a suspicion that the draftsman used the word "deficiency" in 01.09 as synonymous with "defect" in 01.08. On one construction of the orders, order 01.09 was merely completing the process of ensuring that the Master was apprised of all defects. That is how this Court would have interpreted it. But it appears that that is not the way in which order 01.09 was interpreted by

---

130 Investigation into the King's Cross Underground Fire King's Cross Page 146.

deck officers. Masters came to rely upon the absence of any report at the time of sailing as satisfying them that their ship was ready for sea in all respects. That was, of course, a very dangerous assumption.[131]

As senior managers, we can not be expected to know everything. But we should at least assure ourselves that someone is monitoring the important aspects of our business and that they know when to escalate issues, bringing them to our attention.

The belief that the Standing Orders were safe is likely to have driven, or formed the basis of, subsequent decisions. Once a belief takes hold, any of the following assumptions, decisions and behaviours are conditioned by this "anchor". *Anchor bias* is entirely natural but can be dangerous when the original belief or assumption is incorrect. In the case of the Nimrod accident, the belief that the aircraft was safe anyway resulted in a poorly executed safety assessment and ultimately the loss of the aircraft and crew.

First and foremost, as highlighted in chapter 10 A, the NSC [*Nimrod Safety case*] process was fatally undermined by a flawed assumption that the Nimrod was "safe anyway" and that, therefore, the NSC exercise did not really matter. The exercise was seen as merely one of proving something which everyone already knew as a fact, i.e. that the Nimrod was safe. This attitude was corrosive and served to undermine the integrity of the whole NSC process.[132]

As with the team involved in the loss of Nimrod XV230, the NASA management team had been "conditioned by success". This drove them to make some dangerous

131 HERALD OF FREE ENTERPRISE Report of Court No. 8074 Page 12.
132 The Nimrod Review Page 263.

assumptions.

Already, by Friday afternoon, Shuttle Program managers and working engineers had different levels of concern about what the foam strike might have meant. After reviewing available film, Intercenter Photo Working Group engineers believed the Orbiter may have been damaged by the strike. They wanted on-orbit images of Columbia's left wing to confirm their suspicions and initiated action to obtain them. Boeing and United Space Alliance engineers decided to work through the holiday weekend to analyze the strike. At the same time, high-level managers Ralph Roe, head of the Shuttle Program Office of Vehicle Engineering, and Bill Reeves, from United Space Alliance, voiced a lower level of concern. It was at this point, before any analysis had started, that Shuttle Program managers officially shared their belief that the strike posed no safety issues, and that there was no need for a review to be conducted over the weekend. The following is a 4:28 p.m. Mission Evaluation Room manager log entry:

> Bill Reeves called, after a meeting with Ralph Roe, it is confirmed that USA/Boeing will not work the debris issue over the weekend, but will wait till Monday when the films are released. The LCC constraints on ice, the energy/speed of impact at +81 seconds, and the toughness of the RCC[133] are two main factors for the low concern. Also, analysis supports single mission safe re-entry for an impact that penetrates the system. *[USA=United Space Alliance, LCC=Launch Commit Criteria].*[134]

---

133 [Reinforced Carbon-Carbon]
134 Columbia Accident Investigation Board Page 142.

This behaviour is partly due to the previous experience of foam strikes not being an issue, but also the bullish nature of the individuals involved, it would seem.

> **Importance of Communication:** At every juncture of STS-107 [Space Transport System – Flight/mission number], the Shuttle Program's structure and processes, and therefore the managers in charge, resisted new information. Early in the mission, it became clear that the Program was not going to authorize imaging of the Orbiter because, in the Program's opinion, images were not needed. Overwhelming evidence indicates that Program leaders decided the foam strike was merely a maintenance problem long before any analysis had begun. Every manager knew the party line: "We'll wait for the analysis—no safety-of-flight issue expected." Program leaders spent at least as much time making sure hierarchical rules and processes were followed as they did trying to establish why anyone would want a picture of the Orbiter. These attitudes are incompatible with an organization that deals with high-risk technology.[135]

It appears that they viewed those who were concerned about the safety consequences of the foam strike as being unnecessarily conservative and being difficult for the sake of it. It can be very frustrating when people appear to be making things difficult for the sake of it. That frustration can cause some leaders to become entrenched in their position and even more resistant to other views.

Confirmation Bias

NASA operated a meeting system that was designed to encourage discussions about mission safety. Unfortunately,

---

135 Columbia Accident Investigation Board Page 181.

the behaviours of the management team derailed the meeting.

Similarly, Mission Management Team participants felt pressured to remain quiet unless discussion turned to their particular area of technological or system expertise, and, even then, to be brief. The initial damage assessment briefing prepared for the Mission Evaluation Room was cut down considerably in order to make it "fit" the schedule. Even so, it took 40 minutes. It was cut down further to a three-minute discussion topic at the Mission Management Team. Tapes of STS-107[136] Mission Management Team sessions reveal a noticeable "rush" by the meeting's leader to the preconceived bottom line that there was "no safety-of-flight" issue (see chapter 6). Program managers created huge barriers against dissenting opinions by stating preconceived conclusions based on subjective knowledge and experience, rather than on solid data. Managers demonstrated little concern for mission safety. [137]

The purpose of the safety meeting was compromised from the outset. It appears that the management team had made their minds up, so the meeting was simply a tick box exercise. They had become absolutely sure about their theory based on little or no supporting evidence. An assumption was made about a key safety aspect with no relevant information, as was the case in the Herald of Free Enterprise incident.

Mr. Develin appeared to think that the Herald was designed to proceed at sea trimmed 1m by the head, despite the fact that he had no stability information for

---

136 [Space Transport System – Flight/mission number]
137 Columbia Accident Investigation Board Page 192.

the ship in that trim.[138]

In the case of Piper Alpha, "weak signals" were interpreted in a way that strongly confirmed what managers wanted reality to be. In a previous event, handovers and the Permit to Work process were sighted as contributing factors following investigation; senior leaders did not agree.

Mr Richards, who disagreed with the suggestion that there had been a failure in handover or that any deficiency in the operation of the permit system had any bearing on the fatality, said that no changes were made either to handover procedure or the permit system. He considered it important that each person coming on shift was properly informed of what was going on. He said that he would expect all handovers to comprise both a written log and a discussion lasting 10–30 minutes. It was his belief that handover procedures were good and he saw no reason to change them. Handovers were not formally monitored. He did not personally check on their quality but would keep his eye on them. No problems with them had been identified. Mr MacAllan's immediate assessment was that the fatality was due to a structure being used for access and as a walkway when it had not been designed for those purposes. From his experience of working on Piper he was familiar with the routine adopted for handover. He had not checked on handovers during his visits to the platform but "essentially there was a good handover period". Mr McReynolds agreed that the failure to take out a new permit for the change in lifting arrangements was a serious infraction. He said that he had given instructions that separate permits were to be taken out for the rigging component in

138 HERALD OF FREE ENTERPRISE Report of Court No. 8074 Page 29.

maintenance jobs. As far as he was aware everyone was content with the handover system although there was no formal procedure covering it. The information which was passed on seemed adequate and no problems had been identified. He had no concerns about the handover system, but he was not aware that the DEN (Department of Energy) had criticised the shift handover in the case of the Sutherland fatality. Mr Grogan agreed that the change in the scope of the work was a contributory factor to the fatality and that this should not have taken place without the supervisor being informed. He treated this as an aberration of a good system, although there was nothing in the report to support that interpretation. Mr Gordon believed that the complaint related to the handover was ill-founded, but the basis for this was Mr Bodie's assurance that the handover had been well done. His department had not considered handover practice despite the findings of the DEN and Occidental's plea of guilty. The report had highlighted that supervisors must approve any change in the scope of the job. However, this had not alerted him to question the scope of what was covered by the permit in that case.[139]

This tendency to look for information that supports our view or to interpret data in a way that supports what we want to be true is not uncommon. It is referred to as *confirmation bias* and is often an unconscious act. In the case of Columbia, however, it appears that it was actively done.

The opinions of Shuttle Program managers and debris and photo analysts on the potential severity of the debris strike diverged early in the mission and

139 The Public Inquiry Into the Piper Alpha Disaster Volume 1 Page 232.

continued to diverge as the mission progressed, making it increasingly difficult for the Debris Assessment Team to have their concerns heard by those in a decision-making capacity. In the face of Mission managers' low level of concern and desire to get on with the mission, Debris Assessment Team members had to prove unequivocally that a safety-of-flight issue existed before Shuttle Program management would move to obtain images of the left wing. The engineers found themselves in the unusual position of having to prove that the situation was unsafe—a reversal of the usual requirement to prove that a situation is safe.

Other factors contributed to Mission managements' ability to resist the Debris Assessment Team's concerns. A tile expert told managers during frequent consultations that strike damage was only a maintenance-level concern and that on-orbit imaging of potential wing damage was not necessary. Mission management welcomed this opinion and sought no others. This constant reinforcement of managers' pre-existing beliefs added another block to the wall between decision-makers and concerned engineers.

Another factor that enabled Mission managements' detachment from the concerns of their own engineers is rooted in the culture of NASA itself. The Board observed an unofficial hierarchy among NASA programs and directorates that hindered the flow of communications. The effects of this unofficial hierarchy are seen in the attitude that members of the Debris Assessment Team held. Part of the reason they chose the institutional route for their imagery request was that without direction from the Mission Evaluation Room and Mission Management Team, they felt more comfortable with their own chain of command, which was outside the Shuttle Program. Further, when asked by investigators why they were not more vocal about their concerns, Debris Assessment Team members opined that by raising contrary points of view about Shuttle mission safety, they would be singled out for possible ridicule by their peers and managers.

Communication did not flow effectively up to or down from Program managers. As it became clear during the mission that managers were not as concerned as others about the danger of the foam strike, the ability of engineers to challenge those beliefs greatly diminished. Managers' tendency to accept opinions that agree with their own dams the flow of effective communications.

In all official engineering analyses and launch recommendations prior to the accidents, evidence that the design was not performing as expected was reinterpreted as acceptable and non-deviant, which diminished perceptions of risk throughout the agency.[140]

The NASA team had silenced their oversight functions. They were missing their "critical friend". Had they done the most basic verification, it is highly likely that it would have been obvious that all was not well.

Trust But Verify

We must trust our people, of that there can be no doubt. However, that does not mean abdicating responsibility. We must have a mechanism to verify that the trust given is best placed: "Trust but verify." This is about setting yourself up to know when things are not going well so that you can offer support and/or leadership to those who follow you. In the case of London Underground, it appears they did not.

140 Columbia Accident Investigation Board Page 196.

Dr Ridley has recognised that in the past there was a tendency to "management by memo", whereby situations were reported without any follow-up. The Court heard from witnesses numerous examples of failures to communicate effectively between management. As a result, information and analysis often did not reach the people who needed to know. When responsibilities were delegated there was no follow-up to monitor performance, and important responsibilities fell between the gaps of different departments.

Above all, the ordering of priorities and decisions made by the Board were open to doubt because the failure of communication had led to incomplete information reaching them. [141]

Information is naturally filtered, but this means that key information may not reach the decision-makers. Communications channels and KPIs need to be set up to ensure that the information required to make decisions reaches the decision-makers. In many situations, senior managers expect the information to come to them; it is, however, a good idea to conduct validation or verification from time to time.

The organizational structure and hierarchy blocked effective communication of technical problems. Signals were overlooked, people were silenced, and useful information and dissenting views on technical issues did not surface at higher levels. What was communicated to parts of the organization was that O-ring erosion and foam debris were not problems. Structure and hierarchy represent power and status. For both Challenger and Columbia, employees' positions in

---

141 Investigation into the King's Cross Underground Fire King's Cross Page 127.

the organization determined the weight given to their information, by their own judgment and in the eyes of others. As a result, many signals of danger were missed. Relevant information that could have altered the course of events was available but was not presented.[142]

Had the NASA managers verified the information via a process or simple questioning, they may have found that they were not receiving the required information. A simple "go, look, see" can be very powerful and may have resulted in the discovery of the safety shortfalls which caused the Piper Alpha incident.

The safety personnel on the platform and their superiors onshore were in no doubt as to the importance of the systematic giving of induction training at the earliest opportunity when a "newcomer" arrived at the platform. Mr F. McGeogh who had been Safety Training Co-Ordinator with Occidental since February 1988 said that he had received favourable comments from supervisors as to the quality of the induction provided by Occidental. Mr Robertson said that checks were made about every 2 months to ensure that induction was being properly carried out. By this he meant making enquiries of the medic who was responsible for passing the information on the telex to safety personnel. He also said that he had checked with safety personnel that they were going to the lifeboats and the life rafts with the "newcomers". However, he had not checked on the extent to which the inductions were being completed and he had not asked the "newcomers" what they had received.[143]

---

142 Columbia Accident Investigation Board Page 201.
143 The Public Inquiry Into the Piper Alpha Disaster Volume 1 Page 213.

The induction training was very important. It was intended to provide important safety information to those new to the rig. In this case, he asked those who were supposed to give the inductions if they were doing them. If they were the types of people who would not do them despite their importance to safety, they would be unlikely to admit that they were not doing their job. In this case, he trusted them but did not verify. Both are key aspects of safety management.

Abdication of Responsibility

Poor management of safety occurs when we do not show the required level of interest in something which is fundamentally our responsibility. As a senior leader, safety is my responsibility.

> Accidents are indications of failure on the part of management and that, whilst individuals are responsible for their own actions, only managers have the authority to correct the attitude, resource and organisational deficiencies which commonly cause accidents.[144]

I once attended a meeting discussing safety issues that had occurred. The language was very "them" and "they" focused. I tried to explain that "we" and "I" should take a look at ourselves before placing blame on others and that often accidents and events are the fault of management. I will never forget the response from one very senior manager: "When did safety become management's responsibility?" I was astounded, and yet I have discovered that it is not uncommon to find that managers do not understand that safety is ultimately their responsibility. Either they do not understand or do not wish to acknowledge that they have

---

144 The Nimrod Review Page 181.

vital leadership obligations, as was the case in the Herald of Free Enterprise accident.

At first sight the faults which led to this disaster were the aforesaid errors of omission on the part of the Master, the Chief Officer and the assistant bosun, and also the failure by Captain Kirby to issue and enforce clear orders. But a full investigation into the circumstances of the disaster leads inexorably to the conclusion that the underlying or cardinal faults lay higher up in the Company. The Board of Directors did not appreciate their responsibility for the safe management of their ships. They did not apply their minds to the question: What orders should be given for the safety of our ships? The directors did not have any proper comprehension of what their duties were. There appears to have been a lack of thought about the way in which the Herald ought to have been organised for the Dover/Zeebrugge run. All concerned in management, from the members of the Board of Directors down to the junior superintendents, were guilty of fault in that all must be regarded as sharing responsibility for the failure of management. From top to bottom the body corporate was infected with the disease of sloppiness. This became particularly apparent from the evidence of Mr A. P. Young, who was the Operations Director and Mr. W. J. Ayers, who was Technical Director. As will become apparent from later passages in this Report, the Court was singularly unimpressed by both these gentlemen. The failure on the part of the shore management to give proper and clear directions was a contributory cause of the disaster. This is a serious finding which must be explained in some detail.[145]

---

145 HERALD OF FREE ENTERPRISE Report of Court No. 8074 Page 14.

We see a similar failure to verify that practices "in the field" were as they were expected to be. Key safety lessons from a significant incident in another BP facility were issued to the business units. However, they were not followed up to ensure that effective actions were taken to ensure that they were not repeated in other plants. Some of the shortfalls were repeated in Texas City.

BP and the U.K. Health and Safety Executive concluded from their Grangemouth investigations that preventing major accidents requires a specific focus on process safety. BP Group leaders communicated the lessons to the business units, but did not ensure that needed changes were made.[146]

Again, in the case of the Herald of Free Enterprise, we see that another important aspect of safety, watertight integrity, was not given the respect and consideration it was due to close the loop on concerns.

On that memorandum was written:

Tony,

Please submit request to marine department on the usual application

form. If it receives their blessing I will proceed with the specification. It can be done, but will require a few deck and bulkhead penetrations.

On the 13th October 1986 Captain de Ste Croix submitted a job specification for modifications in these terms:

Bridge indication is required to show whether the G

---

146 U.S. CHEMICAL SAFETY AND HAZARD INVESTIGATION BOARD INVESTIGATION REPORT. REPORT NO. 2005-04-I-TX REFINERY EXPLOSION AND FIRE TEXAS CITY, TEXAS MARCH 23, 2005 Page 155

deck bow and stern w/t[147] doors are in the secure or insecure mode.

On this specification Mr. Alcindor wrote:

Please write up preliminary specification for pricing.

On the 18th October 1986 Mr. R. W. King sent a memorandum to Mr. Alcindor in which he said:

I cannot see the purpose or the need for the stern door to be monitored on the bridge, as the seaman in charge of closing the doors is standing by the control panel watching them close.

On the 21st October 1986 Mr. Alcindor sent a memorandum to Captain de Ste Croix which I will quote in full:

Bow and stern door remote indication Reference the Rec./Rep. submitted for the above and Mr. King's specification. I concur in part with Mr. King's penultimate paragraph that the project is unnecessary and not the real answer to the problem. In short, if the bow or stern doors are left open, then the person responsible for closing them should be disciplined. If it is still considered that some modification is required then a simple logic system, e.g. if the clam doors are open and the inner watertight doors closed then the door insecure alarm operates. The stern door on the other hand is visible from within the vehicle deck at all times, therefore the problem should not arise. So in conclusion, the Bridge indication is a "no go."

---

147 [watertight]

On the 28th October 1986, Captain de Ste Croix wrote a further memorandum to masters in which he said:

> Ron King has misjudged my requirements by submitting the attached specification. I consider that bridge indication is required for bow and stern W/T doors due to their extreme importance. He obviously thought I meant the outer bow doors because they cannot be seen when the inner bow doors are closed. Before I go back into print could I please have everyone's opinion? Do we all agree that it is required? To have bridge indication would be very expensive. Would indication on the mooring decks be sufficient? Ideas please.[148]

The focus on disciplining an individual misses the point that the consequences of the doors being open would render a disciplinary hearing the least of their problems. It is also a good example of blaming the individual when there are quite clearly systemic issues at play here. One person falling asleep should not result in 193 fatalities.

---

148 HERALD OF FREE ENTERPRISE Report of Court No. 8074 Pages 24 and 25.

Chapter 6
The Disease of Sloppiness

In this chapter, we will explore the effect of failing to implement or follow our own processes at senior leader level. We will also look at using the regulator, or similar oversight function, to tell us that we are safe, as opposed to taking ownership of safety assurance.

In high-hazard environments, those who are close to the hazard are expected to conduct their work with high levels of professionalism and rigour. This should apply to all of the workforce, including senior leaders. Even the most professional worker can be set up to fail if, for instance, the arrangements that are in place to support them in safely completing their work are not implemented correctly. In many instances, there is nothing wrong with the procedures or management arrangements, but they have not been implemented and tested.

<u>Failure to Implement and Test Arrangements</u>

DuPont was famous for its safety management system. It was viewed as one of the best in class and was sold to other companies. Unfortunately, in the case of the La Porte facility, the system had not been effectively implemented.

[T]his section discusses how DuPont integrated and implemented the frameworks provided by PSM[149], RMP[150], and Responsible Care into its own corporate

149 [Process Safety Management]
150 [Risk Management Plan]

safety management system. Ultimately, this PSM system governed operations at the DuPont La Porte facility at the time of the November 2014 incident (Section 5.4). DuPont La Porte's ineffective implementation of the PSM standard, the RMP rule, Responsible Care, and DuPont's corporate process safety management system resulted in numerous process safety deficiencies that led to the incident. The incident prompted OSHA[151] and the EPA[152] to investigate the DuPont La Porte site and resulted in each of these agencies initiating enforcement actions for alleged violations of federal process safety regulations. The November 2014 incident also caused both ACC[153] and DuPont to evaluate and make changes to their process safety management systems.[154]

This situation was not limited to the La Porte facility. It was found to exist in a number of DuPont plants, which suggests that the senior leadership team was not effective in ensuring that the processes were implemented company-wide.

Despite having robust written process safety management programs (i.e., MOC[155] and PHA[156]), over the course of five years, DuPont had major process safety incidents—including those at its Belle, West Virginia; Buffalo, New York; and La Porte, Texas sites, each of which resulted in fatalities. The CSB[157] found that DuPont La Porte's ineffective implementation of its integrated process safety management system

151 [U.S. Occupational Safety and Health Administration]
152 [U.S. Environmental Protection Agency]
153 [American Chemical Council]
154 Toxic Chemical Release at the DuPont La Porte Chemical Facility Page 60.
155 [Management of Change]
156 [Process Hazard Analysis]
157 [U.S. Chemical Safety and Hazard Investigation Board]

contributed to the severity of the highly toxic material release in the manufacturing building at La Porte.[158]

It can be easy to explain away individual events. It is not until a view is taken across what could be viewed as isolated incidents that patterns emerge and links are made. Their KPIs, audits and other data feeds should have highlighted that the implementation was poor. Each of the safety-significant events over the five-year period across multiple business units could be explained away as a specific problem relating to the business unit that had the last occurrence. Another way of looking at it is that if there are similar occurrences in different business units, the processes or implementation of the processes may be at fault.

In the case of Imperial Sugar, the senior leaders also had many indications that they had significant shortfalls in the implementation of their safety arrangements.

Written housekeeping policies included planned daily, weekly, and monthly packaging area cleaning schedules, but workers reported that these policies were not effectively implemented. Pre-incident photographs of equipment and packaging areas, worker injury reports in 2006 and 2007, and a December 2007 quality assurance survey provided evidence that the housekeeping practices were inadequate—deep piles of spilled granulated and powdered sugar accumulated around and on equipment, and sugar dust accumulated on floors, equipment, and other elevated horizontal surfaces. Workers interviewed by the CSB investigators reported cleaning activities were seldom performed on hard-to-reach elevated surfaces and some powdered

---

158 Toxic Chemical Release at the DuPont La Porte Chemical Facility Page 79.

sugar packaging areas frequently had dense sugar dust in the air.[159]

Despite these shortfalls and the potential cumulative effect, leaders did not take significant action to ensure that their arrangements were robustly implemented. DuPont and Imperial Sugar were not alone in failing to implement and test their own arrangements effectively. The same situation existed on Piper Alpha.

> The system which I have outlined above enabled line management, with the support of the Loss Prevention Department, to carry out its safety responsibility. It provided a system which should have been adequate for the purposes of securing that appropriate safety and emergency equipment and procedures were in place and working as they should. I do not fault Occidental's policy or organisation in relation to matters of safety. However, in previous chapters I have had to consider a number of shortcomings in what existed or took place on Piper. This calls in question the quality of Occidental's management of safety, and in particular whether the systems which they had for implementing the company policy on safety were being operated in an effective manner.[160]

Testing the implementation of arrangements often highlights unforeseen issues. When writing an instruction, for example, what appears to be abundantly clear to the person producing the document can cause confusion or be unachievable at the workplace.

> Two operators (Operator 2 and Operator 3) who were in the control room and heard the distress call ran to

---

159 INVESTIGATION REPORT. Report No. 2008-05-I-GA September 2009 SUGAR DUST EXPLOSION AND FIRE Page 46.
160 The Public Inquiry Into the Piper Alpha Disaster Volume 1 Page 224.

the manufacturing building to help. Another operator (Operator 4) saw Operator 2 and Operator 3 running to the manufacturing building, and he followed them. None of these operators knew of the major release of toxic methyl mercaptan inside of the manufacturing building; therefore, they did not wear any respiratory protection when they ran into the manufacturing building. The manufacturing building lacked automatic visual or audible alarms to alert fieldworkers or prevent them from entering a potentially toxic atmosphere.

In addition, the building's ventilation fans were not working, a situation that, in DuPont's operating procedures, required "restricted access" to the building. But DuPont La Porte's procedures did not define "restricted access" or require that operators wear respiratory protection in the building when access was restricted, even though a toxic chemical release could accumulate in the unventilated building.[161]

Procedures written from behind a desk and not tested often fall short. I was leading a large business unit and, having conducted a field observation, had a feeling that operator rounds were not being conducted correctly.

I visited one of my plants and spoke with the team leader in charge of those who conducted the rounds. I asked him what he did with the output from the completed rounds. He went red with embarrassment. I didn't press the issue any further with him. (That would come later.) I continued my investigation; I conducted an operator round as an operator would. It was a massive eye-opener for me. The procedure had me back and forth between rooms and up and down the same ladders multiple times, and much

---

161 Toxic Chemical Release at the DuPont La Porte Chemical Facility Page 18.

of the equipment was not in the places stipulated in the document. In short, the operator round was not worth the paper it was written on. The team leader didn't do anything with the information that should have come back to him, and the leaders never checked.

Based on all of this, I could easily see how a group of individuals who were expected to conduct this activity twice per day would just sign it off as complete, having done nothing. This situation had existed for years and was a result of a lack of rigour in leadership. We had, unwittingly, fallen into a "do as I say, not as I do" situation as we expected those who were below us to follow procedures and do as they were told, but we had not played our part.

Leaders Failing to Follow Procedures

This failure to do what is expected of us or failure to follow procedures as senior leaders, knowingly or otherwise, was a contributory factor in a number of these events.

> NASA managers believed that the agency had a strong safety culture, but the Board found that the agency had the same conflicting goals that it did before Challenger, when schedule concerns, production pressure, cost-cutting and a drive for ever-greater efficiency—all the signs of an "operational" enterprise—had eroded NASA's ability to assure mission safety. The belief in a safety culture has even less credibility in light of repeated cuts of safety personnel and budgets—also conditions that existed before Challenger. NASA managers stated confidently that everyone was encouraged to speak up about safety issues and that the agency was responsive to those concerns, but the Board found evidence to the contrary in the responses to the Debris Assessment Team's request for imagery, to the initiation of the

imagery request from Kennedy Space Center, and to the "we were just ▢what-iffing'" e-mail concerns that did not reach the Mission Management Team. NASA's bureaucratic structure kept important information from reaching engineers and managers alike. The same NASA whose engineers showed initiative and a solid working knowledge of how to get things done fast had a managerial culture with an allegiance to bureaucracy and cost-efficiency that squelched the engineers' efforts. When it came to managers' own actions, however, a different set of rules prevailed. The Board found that Mission Management Team decision-making operated outside the rules even as it held its engineers to a stifling protocol. Management was not able to recognize that in unprecedented conditions, when lives are on the line, flexibility and democratic process should take priority over bureaucratic response.[162]

In the Challenger teleconference, a key engineering chart presented a qualitative argument about the relationship between cold temperatures and O-ring erosion that engineers were asked to prove. Thiokol's Roger Boisjoly said, "I had no data to quantify it. But I did say I knew it was away from goodness in the current data base." Similarly, the Debris Assessment Team was asked to prove that the foam hit was a threat to flight safety, a determination that only the imagery they were requesting could help them make. Ignored by management was the qualitative data that the engineering teams did have: both instances were outside the experience base. In stark contrast to the requirement that engineers adhere to protocol and hierarchy was management's failure to apply this criterion to their own

---

162 Columbia Accident Investigation Board Page 202.

activities. The Mission Management Team did not meet on a regular schedule during the mission, proceeded in a loose format that allowed informal influence and status differences to shape their decisions, and allowed unchallenged opinions and assumptions to prevail, all the while holding the engineers who were making risk assessments to higher standards. In highly uncertain circumstances, when lives were immediately at risk, management failed to defer to its engineers and failed to recognize that different data standards – qualitative, subjective, and intuitive – and different processes – democratic rather than protocol and chain of command – were more appropriate.[163]

The two examples above highlight that the same issue that had contributed to the loss of the space shuttle Challenger in 1986 still existed when Columbia was lost in 2003. Although the processes and procedures had been changed, the behaviours of leaders had either reverted to old ways or had not changed at all.

It was management's failure to follow best practice, that they themselves had helped develop, that contributed to the explosion at the Airgas facility.

Airgas management did not implement important aspects of industry safety standards, despite the fact that chemical industry good practice guidance clearly states the need to maintain knowledge and conformance with such standards to maintain a safe facility.

Although Airgas participated in the development of the CGA G-8.3 safety standard, the company is not following important aspects of the standard, including:

163 Columbia Accident Investigation Board Page 201.

- Designing equipment so that nitrous oxide is not released into the work environment from venting (CGA G-8.3–2016, Section 4.4.3);
- Using strainers constructed from high nickel or copper alloys (CGA G-8.3– 2016, Section 5.4);
- Preventing metallic particles from being present in nitrous oxide equipment (CGA G-8.3–2016, Section 5.5);
- Verifying that equipment is bonded and electrically grounded to prevent static electricity from initiating a nitrous oxide decomposition reaction (CGA G-8.3– 2016, Section 5.7, 6.1.3, 7.3.4, and 8.2);
- Preventing heating of equipment above 300 °F by all practical means (CGA G8.3–2016, Section 5.7);
- Providing automatic controls to protect equipment from operating at excessive temperatures (CGA G-8.3–2016, Section 5.7);
- Performing management of change and risk assessments on process modifications (CGA G-8.3–2016, Section 5.10);
- Providing an interlock to ensure proper liquid filling and pump cooling before the pump can start (CGA G-8.3–2016, Section 7.4.3);
- Preventing pumps from operating if they lose prime (CGA G-8.3–2016, Section 5.7);
- Using a pump suction filter with as "little pressure drop as possible" (CGA G8.3–2016, Section 7.4.1);
- Verifying that pump inlet pressure (NPSH)292 meets manufacturer requirements (CGA G-8.3–2016, Section 8.2); and
- Monitoring pump outlet pressure to ensure the pump operates within specified conditions (CGA

G-8.3–2016, Section 8.2).[164]

In the case of the Herald of Free Enterprise, the leadership team knew that those on the ship could not do what was expected of them and yet did nothing to correct the issue.

It is a legal requirement that the Master should know the draughts of his ship and that these be entered in the official log book before putting to sea. (See: Section 68(2) of the Merchant Shipping Act 1970 and the regulations made thereunder.) It was particularly important for the Master of the Herald to know the draught of his ship because of the restriction in the number of passengers which the ship was entitled to carry if her draught exceeded 5.5 m moulded. It was even more important that the forward and aft draughts were read at Zeebrugge because of the necessity to trim the ship by the head in that port in order to load vehicles on to E deck.

Captain Lewry told the Court quite frankly that no attempt had been made to read the draughts of his ship on a regular basis or indeed at all in routine service. Fictitious figures were entered in the Official Log which took no account of the trimming water ballast. These figures, if they had been checked by anyone, would have indicated, incredibly, that the ship always sailed on an even keel. In fact the ship normally left Zeebrugge trimmed, and frequently trimmed by the head. Mr. Develin did not appreciate that the stability of the Herald could be significantly affected if the ship was trimmed by the head. Mr. Develin is a Fellow of the Royal Institution of Naval Architects and has

164 Nitrous Oxide Explosion - Airgas (Air Liquide) Cantonment, Florida August 28, 2016 - U.S. Chemical Safety and Hazard Investigation Board Investigation Report One Killed Report Number: 2016-04-I-FL Issue Date: February 2017 Pages 108 and 109.

been a Government Marine Surveyor in Hong Kong. Accordingly he should have appreciated this. Whether the ship had sailed overloaded before the 6th March 1987 is not known, but seems likely.

The difficulties faced by the Masters are exemplified by the attitude of Mr. Develin to a memorandum dated 24th October 1983 and sent to him by Captain Martin. The relevant passages of that memorandum are as follows:

> For good order I feel I should acquaint you with some of the problems associated with one of the Spirit class ships operating to Zeebrugge using the single deck berths.

> At full speed, or even reduced speed, bow wave is above belting forward, and comes three quarters of the way up the bow door . . . Ship does not respond *so* well when trimmed so much by the head, and problems have been found when manoeuvring.

> As you probably appreciate we never know how much cargo we are carrying, so that a situation could arise that not only are we overloaded by **400** tons but also trimmed by the head by 1.4 m. I have not been able to work out how that would affect our damage stability.[165]

This failure to correct known deviations was also evident in Texas City.

BP Texas City's MOC policy also asserts that the MOC be used when modifying or revising an existing startup procedure, or when a system is intentionally operated outside the existing safe operating limits. Yet

165 HERALD OF FREE ENTERPRISE Report of Court No. 8074 Page 26.

BP management allowed operators and supervisors to alter, edit, add, and remove procedural steps without conducting MOCs[166] to assess risk impact due to these changes. They were allowed to write "not applicable" (N/A) for any step and continue the startup using alternative methods.[167]

Using the Regulator as Your Conscience

Leaders are expected to correct shortfalls or deviations. If they don't, it is unlikely that others will. But even when that oversight role is a formal appointment, leadership behaviours can fall short.

QinetiQ's approach was fundamentally lax and compliant. QinetiQ failed at any stage to act as the independent "conscience" of the IPT[168]. As a result, the "third stool" in the safety process, namely independent assurance, was effectively missing from the Nimrod Safety Case process.[169]

The fact that QinetiQ found itself in the position whereby it was "signing-off" on the BLSC[170] without having seen the actual Reports was due in part to its failure to clarify its role at an early stage and its failure later on to insist on being given sight of relevant documentation at any stage. Matters were allowed to drift. This was a failure of management and leadership. QinetiQ's much vaunted 'Matrix Management System' allowed a situation to develop whereby QinetiQ slid into a position of being prepared to go along with an

166 [Management of Change]
167 U.S. CHEMICAL SAFETY AND HAZARD INVESTIGATION BOARD INVESTIGATION RE-
PORT. REPORT NO. 2005-04-I-TX REFINERY EXPLOSION AND FIRE TEXAS CITY, TEXAS
MARCH 23, 2005 Page 77).
168 [Integrated Project Team]
169 The Nimrod Review Page 262.
170 [Baseline Safety Case]

informal process and give assent without any proper formalities being followed. The fact that QinetiQ was prepared to support the sign-off of the NSC in these circumstances is symptomatic of the twin vices of: (a) a lax attitude to the proper proprieties; and (b) a desire to please the client.[171]

When both company management and regulatory bodies fail to perform, there is little else to prevent an accident, as was the case in the Gulf of Mexico.

The DHSG[172] analysis of the available evidence concerning the Macondo disaster indicates that when given the opportunity to save time and money—and make money—tradeoffs were made by the system operator for the certainty of the measurable thing—production. The perception was that there were no downsides associated with the uncertain, difficult-to-measure thing—failure caused by the lack of sufficient protection. As a result of a concatenation of deeply flawed failure and signal analysis, decision-making, communication, and organizational-managerial processes performed by the primary organizations involved in the Macondo well project, safety was compromised to the point that the blowout occurred with catastrophic effects. The regulatory-governance processes (Federal, State, and local) charged with oversight of these operations did not provide the necessary checks and balances to prevent the disaster.

The DHSG investigation has concluded that those who worked on the Macondo well project did not make conscious, *well-informed*, deliberated decisions to trade safety for money. The analyses of the available evidence

171 The Nimrod Review Page 332.
172 [Deepwater Horizon Study Group]

indicate they were trading something that was in their estimation unlikely for something that was sure. They were trading sure savings in time and money—and perhaps quicker returns on investments—for what they took to be the unlikely possibility of a blowout and its unimagined severe consequences. The risks were erroneously judged to be insignificant. Thus, erroneous tradeoffs between risks (safety) and costs were made and set into place.

Available evidence indicates this crew, the onshore support staffs, and the regulatory agency staffs had never experienced a major accident such as that which unfolded on the *Deepwater Horizon*. This failure was beyond their experience—a "failure of imagination." If so, then it is reasonable to conclude that they were operating in conditions at the Macondo site that they had not fully studied or appreciated.[173]

Even when an oversight function or regulator is effective, the effect of being regulated can result in an unfounded confidence in arrangements.

A situation can develop in which we rely on the regulator to tell us whether we are safe and compliant or not, as opposed to doing our own due diligence. The regulator is not our friend or our audit function. If the regulator finds a significant issue that we did not know about, our internal processes have failed.

It is my fundamental belief that safety cannot be legislated, while recognizing that enough legislation or regulation needs to exist to ensure that minimum standards are maintained.

---

173 Final Report on the Investigation of the Macondo Well Blowout Deepwater Horizon Study Group March 1, 2011 Page 84.

Such regulation should impose a duty on the operator to do everything reasonable to

achieve a safe operation. By and large, safety has to be organized by those who are

directly affected by the implications of failure. These people are in the best position to

determine the detailed measures necessary on their own particular installation to achieve the safety objective. Imposition of detailed requirements cannot anticipate all the variances of differing practice, location, organization and size that exist. In fact, prescriptive regulation or over-detailed guidance may at times result in the overall objective actually being compromised. Innovation, on-going improvement and objectivity will be stifled; and the more prescriptive the regulation the more unclear it is who has the responsibility for total safety. Compliance becomes the overriding objective. Sight is lost of the more realistic and overall intent that all reasonable steps should be taken to achieve the total safety of the installation.[174]

Attaining a "green" rating from a regulator who uses a red, amber, green type scoring system means that we have demonstrated compliance with the regulations. Or, to put it another way, the regulator has taken a snapshot of a part of our process and has determined that in that small area we have not broken the law. I have seen many take great comfort from this and see it as a validation that their entire business is therefore safe. This is a false comfort, as the rating simply means that in the part of our business that has been audited, we have met the bare minimum to

---

174 The Nimrod Review Page 165.

comply. That is like attaining the minimum grade at school to pass, but you celebrate as though it is an A grade.

It is our conclusion that the role that the NRC[175] plays in monitoring operator training contributes little and may actually aggravate the problem. NRC has a limited staff for supervising operator licensing, and many of these do not have actual experience in power plants. Therefore, NRC activities are limited to the administration of fairly routine licensing examinations and the spot checking of requalification exams and training programs. In evaluating the training of operators to carry out emergency procedures, NRC failed to recognize basic faults in the procedures in existence at TMI[176]. Since the utility has the tendency of equating the passing of an NRC examination with the satisfactory training of operators, NRC may be perpetuating a level of mediocrity.[177]

---

175 [U.S. Nuclear Regulatory Commission]
176 [Three Mile Island]
177 Report of the President's Commission on the accident at Three Mile Island Page 23.

Conclusion

Although I have focused on examples from high-hazard environments, the key point of note is that leadership is much more powerful than many people appreciate, both as a force for good and for bad.

Accidents are indications of failure on the part of management and that, whilst individuals are responsible for their own actions, only managers have the authority to correct the attitude, resource and organisational deficiencies which commonly cause accidents.[178]

Leaders create culture. It is their responsibility to change it. Top administrators must take responsibility for risk, failure, and safety by remaining alert to the effects their decisions have on the system. Leaders are responsible for establishing the conditions that lead to their subordinates' successes or failures.[179]

Given the statements above, I believe the themes of decision risk assessment, measuring the wrong things or being misled by what we measure, the abdication of responsibility, failing to do what is expected of a leader, and others covered in this book are applicable in many walks of life.

In reading the accident reports, I was able to draw out lessons and themes which resonated with me and my

---

178 The Nimrod Review Page 181
179 Columbia Accident Investigation Board Page 203.

experience. There will be many other issues and lessons to be gained from the reports when viewed through the personal lens of another individual. Given the personal and situational nature of my view of these events, I have also not attempted to offer solutions. As every situation, viewpoint and context will be unique, my aim was to attempt to replicate the heightened level of awareness of my own actions and behaviours that I gained through this study. For me, this has resulted in two things: at times, I use what I have learned to consciously approach issues and problems with these accidents at the forefront of my mind; at other times, a subconscious presence of the learning becomes conscious in situations which are similar to those described in this book. It is, I suppose, a form of latent awareness.

www.ingramcontent.com/pod-product-compliance
Lightning Source LLC
Chambersburg PA
CBHW050733030426
42336CB00012B/1552